CONCILIUM

CONCILIUM   2003/3

'MOVEMENTS' IN THE CHURCH

Edited by
Alberto Melloni

SCM Press · London

Published by SCM Press, 9–17 St Albans Place, London N1 0NX

ISBN 0 334 03074 9

Printed by Biddles Ltd, Guildford and King's Lynn

Concilium Published February, April, June, October
December

Contents

I. Introduction

Movements. On the Significance of Words

ALBERTO MELLONI

A spectre is haunting the church, the spectre of movements. And there is no agreement on the spectre, on its message, or on the nature of these movements.

These expressions of today have a long history of basic meanings. To some they seem to be the sign of religious rebirth, the victory over secularization, the return of an ordered and confident Catholicism, the prophecy of a Christianity with a charisma related to the institution in either synergy or dialectic, *the* fruit of Vatican II, the effect of a gift of the Spirit (or even of a revelation) which makes the laborious renewal to which the bishops in the Council devoted themselves seem banal. Or, on the contrary, the movements are interpreted as a dangerous infection, the overthrow of territorial Catholicism, the collapse of pastoral care of a Tridentine type, the epiphany of an undiagnosed activist semi-Pelagianism, the ephemeral blaze of a rootless Christian juvenilism, the providential army which the Roman centre will use against the reform of the church.

Those who do not like the movements describe them by resorting to the antiquated vocabulary of heresiology (covetousness, secrecy, ambition, careerism, which are all of doubtful moral character). Those who experience them describe the reality in apophatic terms: they do not think that they can be represented outside the experience of revelation, or stylize them with an ahistorical language which emphasizes their origins and expunges their defects, and describes weighty structures as so minimally transparent towards the gospel that *de facto* they are beyond being questioned and irreformable.

I. Understanding

Each of these approaches and the many intermediate positions can be encountered at every level of the church. Bishops support one thesis or the other, for which theologians and canonists provide materials of analysis and propaganda that in every case can appeal to the papal magisterium or refer to the huge bibliography for or against the movements.[1]

It is not the aim of this issue of *Concilium* to take sides in this debate, which could indicate taking sides in the future conclave;[2] not because it should not or cannot, but because the aim of its reflections – whether historical or theological or canonistic or sociological, depending on those who have been invited to contribute – is primarily to understand. This understanding should try to go beyond the laudable level of taking a census;[3] it should explain the success of those analyses which can be immediately used for apologetics or polemics,[4] but at the same time it should refrain from tilting the plane of history so that all the right and all the wrong accumulates at the feet of the present. And sometimes, as in this case, if it takes account of the reader who has the patience to follow our authors to the end, it will see that awareness destroys simplifications to the degree to which it refines language. Language is the first point from which we must start – and it is also the point from which this issue will begin.

In fact there was agreement between the editors of the review that the topic, proposed by more than one of them in the 2001 meeting in Nijmegen, deserved the attention of our authors and our readers – but what was the subject-matter and what was it to be called? On the one hand some asked whether in the ocean of movements (a fallacious word because it is so indeterminate) the process of the 'sectarianization' of Catholicism should not be isolated and studied: in fact both within the dioceses and on a supranational level, in the territory or in the associations, there is a common tendency to express Christian life in the reciprocal acknowledgment of members, to put into practice simplified codes of communication, to fossilize liturgical language churned out with an inventiveness which is soon distorted into immobility. Why not then dedicate an issue to these multiform 'Catholic sects' in which a discipline of voluntary coercion prevents the exit of members from total and totalizing 'worlds'?[5] On the other hand, however, it was asked how it would be possible to look globally and diachronically at those experiences which define themselves as 'movements'. Was it possible to historicize the expression and its history without remaining victims of the play of mirrors in which such diversity is flattened out in a common reference to the papacy, recognized and reduced to an unwritten office of the laws of citizenship in the church? In the end the choice was for an issue which revolves around the fact that Catholic language today defines 'movements' taken together as experiences which in other historical and canonical climates would be or would have been defined definitively as religions or orders or congregations or institutes or societies: to share out of opportunism or necessity that generic 'cognomen' movements is in fact the new feature, the main reason and the weak point of such experiences. We want here to offer historical, theological, canonistic and sociological analyses of them free from obsequies and devoid of phobias.

II. Origins

It is already a historical and political fact that today the term 'movement' seems to be the best, both for those who attack it and those who defend it. The term 'movement' in fact appears in European political language in 1684 to indicate a collective social agitation,[6] and a Jesuit father Louis Doucin used it in the title of his book *Histoire des mouvements arrivez dans l'Eglise au sujet d'Origène et de sa doctrine* which appeared in Paris in 1700, before it was employed in a transferred meaning in connection with the development of philosophical ideas and literary tastes. 'Movement' became established as a synonym of revolution, agitation,[7] but was consecrated by the French political jargon of the Restoration. After July 1830 an opposition between the party of movement and the party of resistance came into being.[8] The use of the term in ecclesiastical debate is different but not independent: the term 'movement' was added to 'Oxford' to indicate the thrust of the spiritual and theological reform which was to be embodied from 1833 in the Tracts for the Times and which, as defined by Jules Gandon in 1844, was identified with the personal story of John Henry Newman.[9] At the level of scientific analysis it was Comte who introduced the term for his quest for a general law of social movement, and L. Stein applied it to the organization of socialism and communism.[10] For Marx and Engels, in fact the movement is the opposite to the élitist organization, and from there, through nineteenth-century sociology,[11] the term passed to twentieth-century political history – which runs from Carl Schmitt (for whom the movement is the accord that unifies people and state[12]) to the definition of Eric Hobsbawm, who called 'movement' the spontaneous element of revolution.[13] Thus modernity uses the term movement for something that has politics as its context; its content is agitation, its expression is the mass.

The term did not find immediate and universal application in nineteenth-century Catholic culture: if historiography spanning the century made a retrospective investigation of the mediaeval 'movements',[14] there remained a marked need in ecclesiastical erudition to distinguish between those that found institutional approval and those that were condemned as sects.[15] However, from the ecclesiological point of view the church adopted a societal language: it is the *societas perfecta* which asserts the visibility of its own institutions against the modern privatization of the religious.[16] The movement entered the secularized present as a form of political militancy and as a factor of the sphere of the church: the church, which produces a sphere of its own, organizes a 'Catholic movement' whose contours follow a long period in history which, not only in Italy, came to a conclusion with the end of its temporal power on 20 September 1870.[17] With respect to the historiographical distinction of Troeltsch, according to whom the difference between sect and church consists in the fact that one is born in the church but joins a sect, the movement became an experience of asymmetry and, following Lamennais' fundamental intuition, has a twofold mark: it recognizes the inadequacy of the restoration model and offers itself as a process – a 'movement' – with which a current within Catholic public opinion takes on the task of measuring itself against the new element of modernity.[18] Thus intransigence and also the party of papal infallibility, Christian trade unionism and Christian democracy, nostalgia for the monarchy and Marian maximalism, the missionary thrust from Europe and the commitment to the emancipation of women, the identification of the youth as an area of encounter and the apostolate, are (or become) a 'movement'.[19] The varied reaction which brought together circles and classes – from the social works of unified Italy to German association Catholicism which resisted the Kulturkampf thanks to these independent organizations – are a movement.[20] The task and the marker of this movement in the singular – *the* Catholic movement – is to conquer and defend social spaces with varied dimensions and geometries: this justifies the existence of all the associations and qualifies the militant laity in the eyes of the pope, even before the bishops, as an élite to be welcomed and governed. With the encyclical *Il fermo proposito* of June 1905, Pius X closes a long period of spontaneity – and with a decision of general scope, still bound up with Italian-French sectors – described this mobilization as 'Catholic action or the action of Catholics', which was meant to have its natural point of reference in the hierarchy.[21]

Thus the term 'movement' completes the definition of the semantic aspects by establishing different relations with the ecclesiastical institution:[22]

on the one hand there are reform movements which qualify on the basis of theological options and shared objectives, and act by influencing their faithful and the ecclesiastical establishment; membership is informal and the number of members is not very important by comparison with the quality of the ideas. Then there are movements of mobilization which link up with the turning point of Catholic Action of 1905 and act as a mass manoeuvre in relation to the bishops and/or the pope; here membership has a different importance and is at the disposal of the institution as such. Finally other experiences radicalize the model of Catholic Action to attempt an integral experience of church movement, which only in some African forms separate and form an independent church. More often an autonomy develops: in this last case membership is binding, and the number of members forms a critical mass in relation to the objectives. Each of these three forms has its own reading of modernity, which is perceived as a potential, as a battlefield or as a threat to identity.[23] Each develops by antinomy a counter-concept: for a movement like Catholic Action the antagonist is acquiescent indifference to the public marginalization of the religious; the renewal movements reject fission in theology, liturgy or discipline which derives from an identification with a particular historical form as the truth; for the church movement the element of polarity is represented by the Tridentine principle of territoriality in which pastoral care must cover community and people.

These are different ways of being a 'movement', but what they have in common is that they engage in dialogue, not exclusively but mainly, with the younger generation, a protagonist emerging in society and in the church: this segment is addressed not only by the associations of the sector (from the *Gioventù cattolica* of Italy in the middle of the nineteenth century to the German youth movement at the beginning of the twentieth), but also other movements which offer young people identity, models, belonging, values, words of order, ideologies.[24] So by going a little deeper it is possible to identify specific connotations in different movements – while increasingly being led spontaneously to the unspecific identification which is certainly also inspiring exegetical research.[25]

III. Reform movements

Those groups which, following the Oxford Movement, identify an issue on which to exercise political pressure with a view to renewing the Christian churches belong to the group of reform movements. Such movements, which cross all Christian confessions and denominations, do not seek to change the allegiance of their faithful; making them aware of the context by means of a strategy of advocacy, they set out to modify the government of the ecclesiastical institution which they are addressing.[26]

Immediately after this, mention should be made of the liturgical movement. It came from a monastic background and with Dom Prosper Guéranger gave voice to the need to strip the old layers of devotionalism from the Latin liturgy by relating it to its primitive purity. An expression of the culture of restoration, in the course of the twentieth century the liturgical movement took on an essential function, because it unblocked that instinctive identification between truth and immobility that had marked the political and theological culture of intransigence.[27] It raised the question of the ordering of the cult not in the name of a 'progress' but in the name of a 'restoration'. That made it invulnerable to Roman suspicions, and indeed allowed the papal magisterium to accept its proposals step by step.[28]

The movement of a return to the patristic sources was not dissimilar. In this area in particular a group of theologians tried to reintroduce into the rigid scheme of neo-Thomism which dominated the Catholic schools the voice and plurality of Latin and above all Greek antiquity.[29] However, in this sphere the Roman centre became alarmed: as early as 1936–42 the Holy Office issued a condemnation when a young Dominican master proposed that the theology of Thomas should be relocated in its history as a model of a lively and dialectical relationship between time and the gospel.[30] And as a result the protagonists of the related attempt to return to the sources fell silent, a silence broken only with the convening of Vatican II and the new climate created by the Council.[31]

The biblical movement was even more exposed: the idea of being able to apply the historical-critical method to the reading of the scriptures as a gesture of intellectual loyalty towards modern culture and as the force for a new apologetics in keeping with the present time was a position which the Holy See interpreted and repressed as the 'synthesis of all the heresies', modernism.[32] A steady stream of disciplinary measures from the Holy Office made the life of Catholic exegetes very difficult: but the multiplication of journals and areas of research which make up the movement stimulated Roman circles themselves and allowed the survival of interests, competences and thrusts which Pius XII would partly satisfy with the encyclical *Divino afflante spiritu* (1943).[33]

However, the most important and the most exposed of these renewal movements was the ecumenical movement. Originating within the Protestant world, this movement, which had a glimpse of the unity of the church as a possibility and a vocation of Christians in the twentieth century, also gained supporters in the Roman Catholic sphere. Whereas the papacy had accepted and encouraged the 'unionist' pledge to seek to 'bring back' to communion with a Rome which had become paternal and benevolent those who had not removed themselves from it by entering into error, its attitude towards a conception of unity which sought the theological significance of Christian diversity was severe.[34] It was severe towards the Belgian attempts of the 1920s to articulate unity, union and involvement in dialogue; it was severe towards the subsequent participation of Catholics in the movement as such, who in 1928 fell under the inflexible condemnation of the encyclical *Mortalium animos*; and it was most severe of all towards those theologians, like Yves Congar, who sought to discover the principles of a 'Catholic ecumenism', so that the Roman church did not miss this *kairos*.[35]

To this summary list could be added movements with less of an international or interconfessional spread – from the Slavophiles of Orthodox Russia to the Greek Onomatomachi; from movements seeking greater responsibility for the Catholic laity to movements of a political character. However, those mentioned in this first approximate survey can already demarcate an area about which this issue can add nothing to current historiography.

IV. Movements of mobilization

The organization of Catholic associations already appears in Europe between the nineteenth and twentieth centuries as a 'Christian social movement' which frames and forms masses of the faithful.[36] In other cultural universes – we need think only of the Pentecostal revival in the United States – such forms are called sectarian, not as a value judgment but to describe their internal organization and relations with the established churches. However, in Catholic Europe the language of movement became fused with the vocabulary of Catholic Action, a new setting into which the papacy introduced lay mobilization. The Catholic movement (a term which after the Great War was heavily 'occupied' by the self-representations of Fascism and Nazism) describes the historical experience: Catholic Action, comprising millions of people, was, however, protected from above from the rivalry of those who thought of an autonomous political context – like Action Française, condemned in 1926.[37] Two organizational hypotheses competed within it, the Italian model of Catholic Action with sectors divided by age and gender, and the Franco-Belgian model with specialization by background and profession, but the way in which these are implemented was very different.[38] In some countries the formative structure of Catholic Action remained hegemonic and gained ground at the expense of the ancient networks of the confraternities; in others pre-existing realities (like Quickborn or the Grossdeutsche Jugend in Germany) were reintroduced into Catholic Action in the broader sense, groups under the control of the bishops (like the Neudeutschland Bund founded in 1919 by Cardinal Hartmann in Cologne with assistants nominated by the bishops), groups which were a response to cultures very distant from the European schemes of a struggle against secularization (like the American communitarian movement of Dorothy Day).[39]

Within mass Catholic Action, on which totalitarian political power was in a position to impose strong conditions,[40] the idea then arose that 'a new Christian chivalry'[41] was necessary and useful for regaining society for Christ; Catholic Action as such was the breeding ground for its initiation. Experiences became differentiated from the mass, experiences which sought a higher perfection either in intellectual refinement or in the preparation of a Catholic ruling class,[42] or through the theorization of very rigorous spiritual experiences, or in an unprecedented combination of consecration and lay life, or greater recognition of the link between priestly ordination and militant association.[43]

Pius XII had the arduous task of containing and directing all these thrusts. On the one hand he gave a legal framework to the rising 'chivalry': he opened up the secular institutions and gave papal recognition to various of them. On the other hand he had to think of the lay organizations within the parameters of Catholic Action (duties, privileges, dependence). He was guided by a conception of the whole church as a movement: the slow elaboration of this thesis, which sought to be a response to the analyses of the decline of the church and the need to construct a theology of the laity, could be said to have matured when at the World Congress for the Apostolate of the Laity in 1951 he asserted that 'To have the church provided with its own means of guaranteeing its action . . . this was the origin of what are called the Catholic movements which, under the guidance of priests and laity, strengthened by their effective compacts and sincere fidelity, draw along the great mass of believers to the struggle and to victory.' In this church-movement the insecure and timid leader Pacelli became the prophet in whose vision the time was near when 'crowds would overflow every part of the vast St Peter's Square to receive his blessing and listen to his word'.[44]

V. Movements-church

This visionary and excited climate left a deep mark on Catholic Action, exhausted by the excesses of militany,[45] but it was in this very climate that many of the realities came into being which would be included in the term movement at the end of the twentieth century. Arising out of mystical experiences like those of José M. Escrivá, who in 1928 became mediator of what he quite succinctly called Obra de Dios,[46] or in extreme circumstances like those of the priests who followed Marcial Maciel in proclaiming themselves Legionaries of Christ, these movements wanted from the pope something more than being recognized as splinters of Catholic Action.[47] Like the powerful network of the Better World founded by the Jesuit Fr Lombardi after a speech by Pius XII,[48] they did not limit themselves to using the law of associations. Many of them – but not the Focolari, for example[49] – inherited from Catholic Action the capacity to engage in dialogue with an institution which was mistrustful, if not hostile, while at the same time challenging it: but above all they overturned the superimposition of church and movement which was at the heart of Pius XII's vision. Thus from the church-movement there emerged a vision of a movements-church: this radicalized these features within a concrete experience. The chain of command became vertical from the founder; consecration became the sacrament of militancy which involved even married people; the objective of the reconquest of society became the end which justified both the practice of secrecy and extreme visibility; finally, despite the risks already seen with Maurras, direct action was preferred to the slow culture of mediation and the project.[50]

These spiritual experiences, bound up with the charisma of a founder not just of religious congregations but also open to men and women living in the world, used the spiritual and canonical means at their disposal: whereas Fr Lombardi suddenly adopted the figure of the movement, the others described themselves as pious associations, congregations, works, secular institutions, congregations which derived their mentality and style from their culture of reference. It was in fact typical of the 1930s, before Escrivá's Obra de Dios, to believe that a small group of agitators could change the world. And a marked integration with the world of politics was more typical of the Roman fabric in which the old Marian congregations of the Jesuit fathers prospered (between the wars they became Communities of Christian Life and were recognized by Pius XII as a 'type' of Catholic Action[51]). Thus it would be wrong to project retrospectively the same light on other experiences within or against Catholic Action – like the formative module of the

Cursillos de Cristianidad,[52] the family groups which took Catholic Action's vow of sharing between the sexes,[53] the Focolari movement, the Pro sanctitate movement which gathered in Rome around Mgr Giaquinta,[54] and not least the student associations, like Gioventù studentesca, which in Milan referred to Fr Turoldo and Don Luigi Giussani.[55]

VI. The shift at the Council and the reordering of vocabulary

The shift at Vatican II changed the ecclesiological language and the historical and political horizons within which all these worlds had been thought of and defined.

On the one hand the renewal movements were welcomed and all their authorities were reviewed.[56] On the other, Catholic Action had to be rethought, so that its universalistic dimension and direct dependence on the pope which, once again with important nuances, had marked its origin and history, was connected with the promotion of the laity, as 'agents' of the re-Christianization of society, to being members of the people of God, called to baptismal sanctity, human brotherhood.[57] Finally the movements-church born under Pius XII had to rethink its position in a church which had dropped the vision of itself as a movement of movements and had assumed the perspective of the *communio ecclesiarum*.[58] As for the principle of internal association, what prevailed was the emphasis on the charisma of foundation, subject to the pope for a judgment which more resembled the infallibility of the bull of canonization than the empirical reality of the old institution of recognition.[59] And the person of the pope – the physical possibility of attracting his attention which brought out of limbo the Legionaries in 1965, the Neo-Catechumens in 1974 and Communion and Liberation in 1975 – protected the experience from the mistrust of bishops or the Curia.[60]

While the 'agony of the parish' was announced from every corner of the Catholic Church and the reception of the ecclesiology of the local church made progress through thousands of obstacles, these last experiences responded to the cries and the impatience. It was not the only one, but the young group was the protagonist of this stage of foundation and rapid disappearance: the common conviction was that the climate after the council was 'prophetic' and necessitated attempts, researches, adventures with a 'touch of utopia'. The stories are many and diverse – as diverse as the rhythm of growth, the balance between abandonment and recruitment, the relationship with local or Roman ecclesiastical authority, territorial roots, the formalization of militancy, the internal hierarchy, the differentiation of tasks between clergy and laity, the role of the founder, the political commitment, the presence of the generations, the international dissemination, the attitude towards the other churches, the material structures, the attitude towards religious or matrimonial vocations.

There is nothing new from the perspective of events; what is new lies in the proportions, in the representation of this sea of diversity, often in very severe antagonism, under the generic term 'movements'. Certainly this homologization is favoured not only verbally by some transitions which mark the circumstances of the various realities after the Council and during the pontificate of Montini: we need only think of the decision of the Legionaries to settle in Rome; of the privilege of a personal prelature granted to Obra; of the support given by Cardinal Suenens to the Legion of Mary and the charismatic movement; of the numerical success in the recruitment of the vocations of neocatechumens at a time of poverty.[61]

Above all, however, it has been John Paul II who has recognized in this plurality a unitary force which the church needs and which is destined to be amalgamated with it – in practice more than in theology. It is a process which began, in a context in which movements and institutions were aware of their diversity, with the meeting at Rocca di Papa in 1981.[62] From this there emerged a series of colloquia, organized in successive years,[63] which found a focus in the lively debate by the Synod of Bishops in 1987 on the laity in the church:[64] In fact for many bishops the emphasis placed from on high on these groups – even when they did not take a traditional form[65] – made it difficult to give a report. The topic was debated in the Congress of Canon Law in 1989,[66] but then the time was not one of analysis but of polemics, drawing in the politics of canonization.[67]

And in the polemic John Paul II did not cease to support the movements, protagonists of many mobilizations and above all of the ceremony at Pentecost 1998 in which the pope received and solemnized his recognition of the founder of the larger and representative among these movements which met at a congress in Rome: the pope saw them as the leaven of the 'new' evangelization and as a fruit of the Council.[68] The movements, for all their evident diversity and antagonisms, accepted this reciprocal homologization, which guaranteed their visibility, power and protection.

However, the topic continues to provoke lively polemic: among canon lawyers, some of whom hesitate over how to describe the law of the association of the faithful as a privilege which discriminates against those who are 'simply' baptized;[69] among theologians, who are not always disposed to accept the autobiographical descriptions as the *raison d'être* of vexations (which today are rarer) and privileges;[70] among sociologists, who discuss the impossibility of putting the movements into the categories of church or sect or into the more refined categories of the multiplication of what religious products are on offer in the Catholic 'supermarket';[71] among bishops and priests who feel attracted and threatened by a protagonism which some experience has chosen for all;[72]among the militants of the movements themselves, who are forced to relate to a reality which is not homogeneous and regarded as being responsible for all that is imputed to this unnatural conglomeration.

VII. A diverse future

What emerges from this framework which I have just sketched out, and which is meant solely to introduce readers to the work done by the rest of the authors of this issue, is thus that the panorama is unstable and cannot just be reduced to a single cipher.

On the side of the movements, the majority of those which today claim visibility and will perhaps become even more visible as we see a second generation of leaders, it is difficult to say how forms of order and incidences will survive. Despite the kindness of the webmasters of many movements and the Pontifical Council for the Laity, it has been impossible to offer a comparative pattern of recruitment, diffusion and average age of organizations: at all events these are numbers which pale before those of Catholic Action in Milan in the 1930s, of which just over thirty years later little remains. And in any case even beyond the quantum and the physiological risk, the problem remains open of what and how the joint presence of movements which differ in style and spiritual reference will be regulated; the statutes – so different in quality and so eloquent in their diverse ecclesiologies – have not been defined.[73]

On the other hand, also on the side of territorial Catholicism, the mobility of people makes pastoral care a matter of chance; not only does it no longer have rigid boundaries, but it has to be measured against the culture of the clergy and the models of reference which it finds in the papacy and in society. And new movements which cross confessional or cultural divisions – radical pacifism, ecologism, feminism, the anti-globalization archipelago – are again becoming highly visible, in very different contexts.

So if there is a risk of sectarianization,[74] if the motherhood of the church presents itself as a reason for competition between sons and daughters, if in this fissurization the role of the movements is a delicate one, the problem shown by their historical dynamic is greater: the whole of Catholicism which has to decide whether, having crossed the secular threshold and the biblical measure of the forty years since Vatican II, the development of its identity must be that of a great network of sites reserved for a registered clientele, or of an open 'sanctuary', humanizing, hospitable, in which there is – as an inscription on an ancient amphora reads – 'each one with his gift, each one with his burden'.

Translated by John Bowden

Notes

1. P. Pingault, *Renouveau de l'Eglise: les communautés nouvelles*, Paris 1989; G. Cholvy, *Histoire des organisations et mouvements chrétiens de jeunesse en France (XIXe–XXe siècle)*, Paris 1999.

2. A. Melloni, *Il conclave. Storia di una istituzione*, Bologna 2001.

3. *Movimenti ecclesiali contemporanei. Dimensioni storiche, teologico-spirituali ed apostoliche* ed. A. Favale, Rome ²1982. A.Giolo and B. Salvarani, *I cattolici sono tutti uguali? Una mappa dei movimenti della Chiesa*, Genoa 1992, has a very Italian perspective.

4. B. Secondin, *I nuovi protagonisti. Movimenti, associazioni, gruppi nella chiesa*, Cinisello Balsamo 1991.

5. J. A. Beckford, 'Religious organization: a survey of some recent publications', *Archives des sciences sociales des religions*, 1984, 1, pp. 83–102; conversely, note the commitment of the Catholic Alliance, an organization with an ultra-conservative standpoint, to sound alarms about the sects by means of the support and space put at the disposal of the lawyer M. Introvigne, and the activity of Cesnur, on which see www.cesnur.it.

6. As a synonym of *Aufruhr*, cf. J. B. Schuppius, *Lehrreiche Schriften (1684)*, p. 722; quoted by J. Freese in *PhW*; lexicographically, it appears in German in J. C. Adelung, *Grammatisch-kritisches Wörterbuch der hochdeutsch*, I, Mundart 1811, p. 965.

7. C. von Clausewitz, 'Umtriebe', in *Politische Schriften und Briefe*, ed. GGS.

8. J. Frese refers to the entry 'Bewegung und Reaktion', in *Conversations. Lexicon de neuesten Zeit und Literatur* 2, 1832, pp. 245–48. Hegel also spoke of movement in reflecting on the July revolution. F. Goguel, *La politique des partis sous la 3ᵉ République*, Paris 1948, and *La politique en France*, Paris 1981; Goguel observed that this dichotomy could not be maintained in the twentieth century, when resistance took on a positive value.

9. O. Chadwick, *The Spirit of the Oxford Movement*, Cambridge 1990.

10. A. Comte, *Le traité général du progrès humaine*, Paris 1853, ch. I; O. Brunner, W. Conze and R. Koselleck (eds), *Geschichtliche Grundbegriffe. Historisches Lexikon der politisch-sozialen Sprache in Deutschland*, 7 + 2 vols, Stuttgart 1972–84, ad loc., refer to L. Stein, *Der Sozialismus und Communismus des heutigen Frankreichs. Ein Beitrag zur Zeitgeschichte*, which appeared in 1842.

11. Alfred Fouillée, *Le mouvement et la conception sociologique du monde*, Paris 1896.

12. Carl Schmitt, *Staat, Bewegung, Volk, Die Dreigliederung der politisches Einheit*, 1933, now in *Staat, Grossraum, Nomos: Arbeiten aus den Jahren 1916 – 1969*, Berlin 1995.

13. E. J. Hobsbawm, *Sozial-Rebellen. Archäische Sozial-Bewegungen im 19. und 20. Jahrhundert* (1962), Luchterhand ²1971.

14. From the mediaeval historiography personified by E. Demolins, *Le mouvement communal et municipal au Moyen Age*, Paris 1875, to the reception of the narrative of doctrinal development in J. de Ghellinck, *Le mouvement théologique du XIIᵉ siècle*, Paris 1914.

15. B. Plongeron, *L'abbé Grégoire et la République des savants*, Paris 2001, rightly draws attention to Gregoire's *Histoire des sectes religieuses*, which appeared in two volumes in 1814 and was promptly confiscated by Napoleon's police; the work reappeared in 1828 in five volumes, with around 100 pages of *Prolégomènes* in which the learned priest listed around 70 'sects' more or less deriving from Christianity.

16. É. Poulat, *Église contre bourgeoisie*, Paris 1967, further elements in *Liberté – Laïcité. La guerre des deux France et le principe de la modernité*, Paris 1988.

17. E. Vercesi, *Il movimento cattolico in Italia (1870–1922)*, Florence 1923, stands at the beginning of a series which in Italy has also produced a large *Dizionario storico del movimento cattolico in Itali* (3 vols), Genoa 1980–97, ed Giorgio Campanini and Francesco Traniello. For France see Y. Tranvouez, *Catholique d'abord: approches du mouvement catholique en France (XIXe-XXe siècle)*, Paris 1990.

18. G. Verucci, *Félicité Lamennais. Dal cattolicesimo autoritario al radicalismo democratico*, Bologna 1977.

19. G. Cholvy (ed), *Mouvements de jeunesse chrétienne et juifs. Societé juvénile dans un cadre européen, 1799–1868*, Paris 1985; for the Italian perspective see D. Veneruso, 'La Gioventù Cattolica e i problemi della società civile e politica italiana dall'Unità al Fascismo (1867–1922)', in *La 'Gioventù Cattolica' dopo l'Unità 1866–1968*, Rome 1972, pp. 1–137.

20. Cf. *Il Kulturkampf in Italia e nei paesi di lingua tedesca* ed R. Lill and F. Traniello, Bologna 1992.

21. For the entanglement of the Opera dei congressi in 1904 and the birth of the three unions (popular, electoral and socio-economic) following *Il fermo proposito* of 1905, cf. L. Ferrari, *Una storia dell'Azione cattolica: gli ordinamenti statutari da Pio IX a Pio XII*, Genoa 1988.

22. Against the establishment (which became a possible counter-concept), it is present at the birth of movements of a Pentecostal kind, and new churches like those of the African prophets, on which see A. Hastings, *A History of African Christianity 1950–1975*, Cambridge ²1986.

23. A. Riccardi, *Intransigenza e modernità. La chiesa cattolica verso il terzo millennio*, Rome and Bari 1996.

24. W. Laqueur, *Die deutsche Jugendbewegung: eine historische Studie*, Cologne 1983, and *La 'Gioventù Cattolica' dopo l'Unità 1866–1968*, Rome 1972; for France see Cholvy, *Histoire des organisations et mouvements chrétiens de jeunesse en France* (n. 19). For the scouts cf. C. Chabrier, *L'adoption du scoutisme par l'Eglise catholique en France, pendant l'entre-deux-guerres: pour des Scouts catholiques ou des Catholiques scouts?*, Sorbonne dissertation 1995.

25. For the views of G. Theissen, *The Sociology of the Jesus Movement* (American title)/*The First Followers of Jesus* (English title), Philadelphia and London 1978, see the article by Claudio Gianotto below (pp. 33f.).

26. É. Fouilloux, *Une église en quête de liberté: la pensée catholique française entre modernisme et Vatican II*, Paris 1998, and *Au coeur du XXᵉ siècle religieux*, Paris 1993.

27. G.-M. Oury, *Dom Guéranger. Moine au coeur de l'Eglise*, Sablé-sur-Sarthe 2000.

28. Cf. M. Paiano, *Liturgia e società nel Novecento. Percorsi del movimento liturgico di fronte ai processi di secolarizzazione*, Roma 2000.

29. É. Fouilloux, *La collection 'Sources Chrétiennes'. Éditer les Pères de l'Église au XXᵉ siècle*, Paris 1995.

30. Cf. M.-D. Chenu, *Le Saulchoir. Une école de théologie* ed G. Melloni, Paris 1985.

31. Cf.G. Alberigo (ed), *History of the Second Vatican Council*, I, Maryknoll 1996ff. (4 vols).

32. P. Colin, *L'audace et le soupçon: la crise dans le catholicisme français 1893–1914*, Paris 1997.

33. M. Pesce, 'Dalla enciclica biblica di Leone XIII "Providentissimus Deus" (1893) a quella di Pio XII "Divino Afflante Spiritu" (1943)' in C. M. Martini, G. Ghibberti and M. Pesce, *Cento anni di cammino biblico*, Milan 1995, pp. 39–100.

34. Cf. E. Fouilloux, *Les catholiques et l'unité chrétiénne du XIXᵉ au XXᵉ siècle. Itinéraires européennes d'expression française*, Paris 1982.

35. Cf. R. Loonbeek and J. Mortiau, *Un pionnier, dom Lambert Beauduin (1873–1960). Liturgie et Unité des chrètiens*, Louvain-la-Neuve 2001, and *Cardinal Yves Congar (1904–1995)*, ed A. Vauchez, Paris 1999.

36. Cf. Tiziano Veggian, *Il movimento sociale cristiano nella seconda metà di questo secolo*, Vicenza 1899.

37. J. Prévotat, *Les catholiques et l'Action française. Histoire d'une condamnation (1899–1939)*, Paris 2001.

38. In 1924 Cardijn founded the Jeunesse Ouvrière Chrétienne in Belgium, which was soon followed by its French twin, and then appeared in Spain, cf. M. A. Walckiers, *Sources inédites relatives aux débuts de la Joc, 1919–1925*, Louvain 1970, and J. Balenciaga, 'Aux origines de la Joc en Espagne. Le rôle de Valladolid' in Cholvy, *Mouvements de jeunesse chrétienne et juifs* (n. 19), pp. 269–88. JOC remained the only youth movement active in the Association catholique de la Jeunesse Française and its Belgian equivalent; however, a professional specialization developed in Catholic Action which saw the rise of Jeunesse Agricole Catholique (1929) and Jeunesse Étudiante Chrétienne (1930), then followed by sections for sailors, the independents and in 1935–39 the leagues of Catholic workers (LOCF e LOC), which in 1942 were to give life to the Mouvement Populaire de Familles. The ecclesiastical mandate of this movement was withdrawn in 1946; in 1949 it was declared outside the church and a movement of pro-communist liberation. The origin of the Hermanedades de Obreros de Acción Católica in Spain in 1941 also created tension with the bishops, especially as from the end of the 1940s and beginning of the 1950s, HOAC adopted a clear anti-capitalist position. In Germany the German branch of JOC, the Christliche Arbeiterjugend, was formed in 1949, in very different circumstances.

39. In 1933 Dorothy Day and Peter Maurin founded the Catholic Workers Movement, which preached an inner conversion for the communitarian revolution. Cf. J. P. Dolan, *The American Catholic Experience. History from Colonial Times to the Present*, Garden City 1985, pp. 409–17.

40. Nazism rejected all this in the parish and in 1945 allowed the bishops to impose the *Pfarrprinzip* in place of the *Verbandsprinzip*, giving the national structures the nature of federations of parochial associations.

41. J.-M. Mayeur, 'Forme di organizzazione del laicato cattolico', in *I cattolici nel mondo contemporaneo 1922–1958, Storia della chiesa XXIII* ed E. Guerriero and F. Traniello, Cinisello Balsamo 1991, p. 485.

42. R. Moro, *La formazione della classe dirigente cattolica (1929–1937)*, Bologna 1979; id., 'La storiografia sulla FUCI: bilancio e prospettive', in *Alla ricerca delle storie della FUCI*, Ricerca 13, 1997, nos 10–12, 25–8.

43. J. Kwiatkowski, *Gli Istituti Secolari nei documenti precodiciali e nella legislazione canonica attuale*, Rome 1994. With *Provida Mater*, Pius XII was to act on the suggestions made to him by Fr Agostino Gemelli – the founder of the Catholic Univeristy of Milan – and open the door to these organizations.

44. A. Riccardi, 'La chiesa di Pio XII educatrice di uomini e di popoli tra certezze e crisi' in *Chiesa e progetto educativo nell'Italia del secondo dopoguerra*, Brescia 1988, pp. 9–36, also for the quotation from *Discorsi e Radiomesaggi*, Vol. 13, 1950, pp. 293–301 and from the discussion on French TV of 17 April 1949, ibid., Vol. 11, pp. 45–47. The diary by the ambassador F. Charles-Roux, *Huits ans en Vatican, 1932–1940*, Paris 1947, p. 72, gives the impression of timidity.

45. The symbol of this in Italy is Luigi Gedda, on whom see G. Alberigo, 'Gedda ieri . . . e anche oggi?', *Cristianesimo nella storia* 21, 2000, pp. 687–94.

46. John Paul II to Opus Dei, 11 August 1979. Born in Aragon in 1902, Josemaría Escrivá de Balaguer had a vision in 1928 of a movement of the 'sanctification of ordinary things'. This took its name only in 1930, when a woman's branch was also formed. The Società sacerdotale della santa Croce was formed in February 1943 and approval arrived from Rome on 8 December 1943. From 1946 Escrivá came to Rome (1947 *decretum laudis* and 1950 definitive approval).

47. In *Dizionario degli Istituti di perfezioni* (5 vols), Rome 1978, s.v., see also *New Catholic Encyclopedia – Jubilee Volume*, Detroit 2001, s.v.

48. Cf. G. Zizola, *Il microfono di Dio. Pio XII, p. Lombardi e i cattolici italiani*, Milan 1990.

49. There is autobiographical testimony in F. Zambonini, *Chiara Lubich: l'avventura dell'Unità*, Alba 1991.

50. P.Chenaux, *Entre Maurras et Maritain: une génération intellectuelle catholique*, Paris 1999.

51. From the Marian congregation founded by Jean Leunis in the Roman College around 1563 and recognized by Gregory XIII as a primary congregation; on the suppression of the Society in 1773, Clement authorized the survival of the congregations; only in 1922 did the General organize a central secretariat, which was consecrated with the *Bis sæculari* of 27 September 1948. After the Lay Congress of 1950, work was done on the new statutes, approved in the course of the same year (papal approval came in 1953); the request for a single rule was granted with the general principles approved by Paul VI in 1968 and 1971 which created the Community of Christian Life (referred to as CVX); cf. F. Botta, 'Le comunità di vita cristiana' in *Movimenti ecclesiali contemporanei. Dimensioni storiche, teologico-spirituali ed apostoliche* ed A. Favale, Rome 1982, pp. 115–29; E. Villaret, *Les Congrégations Mariales*, Paris 1947.

52. The Cursillo formed in 1940 and developed in the circles of Catholic Action of Mallorca in 1948–49 in response to the call of Pius XII: here too it was a bishop, Hervás y Benet, who after the pilgrimage of 100,000 young people to Santiago launched the first Cursillo: after 1953 it spread.

53. Family movements: Domus christianae founded by Don Giovanni Rossi in 1939; groups of family spirituality founded by Mgr Carlo Colombo in 1961; the Équipes Notre-Dame, founded by Henry Caffarel in 1939; the Movimiento Familiar Cristiano promoted by Llorente and by Fr Pedro Rihards, a Passionist, in Buenos Aires in 1948; the Movimento di Rinascita Cristiana, founded by Albert Dauchy in Rome in 1943; cf. T. Bertone, 'Movimenti di spiritualità e apostolato familiare' in *Movimenti ecclesiali contemporanei. Dimensioni storiche, teologico-spirituali ed apostoliche*, ed A. Favale, Rome ²1982, pp. 132–52.

54. The Pro sanctitate movement, formed in Rome in 1947 on the initiative of Mgr Guglielmo Giaquinta, Bishop of Tivoli

55. There is a reconstruction orientated on the rise of the following movement in M. Camisasca, *Comunione e Liberazione. Le origini (1954–1968)*, Milan 2001.

56. É. Fouilloux, 'Mouvements théologico-spirituels et concile (1959–1962)' in *À la veille de Concile Vatican II. Vota et réactions en Europe et dans le Catholicisme oriental* ed M. Lamberigts and C. Soetens, Louvain 1992, pp. 185–99.

57. J. Ratzinger, *Popolo e casa di Dio in Sant'Agostino*, Milan 1975.

58. The richest and most complex reflection is that now collected in the two volumes by Eugenio Corecco, *Ius et communio. Scritti di diritto canonico*, Asti 1997.

59. Id., 'Profili istituzionali dei movimenti nella chiesa' in *I movimenti nella chiesa degli anni '80*, pp. 203–34: for Corecco, the movement is the expression of a charism, as the church is the expression of the institution. L. Gerosa, 'Le charisme originaire. *Pour une justification théologique du droit d'association dans l'Eglise*', *Nouvelle Revue Théologique* 112, 1990, pp. 224–35, does not draw such a clear line.

60. For the protest movement cf. S. Tarrow, *Democrazia e disordine. Movimenti di protesta e politica in Italia 1963–1975*, Bari 1990, who devotes a good deal of space to Catholic dissent.

61. P. Zimmerling, *Die charismatischen Bewegungen. Theologie – Spiritualität – Anstosse zum Gespräch*, Göttingen 2001.

62. [Pontifical Council for the Laity], *Première rencontre des mouvements qui promeuvent la vie spirituelle des laïcs. Rocca di Papa 14–18 avril 1980*, Vatican City 1981. For the differences see A. Gilberto, 'Movimenti ecclesiali e istituti secolari: una realtà da ascoltare', *Presbyteri*, 1980, pp. 406–13. Also D. Grasso, 'I movimenti carismatici e gli istituti secolari' in *Carisma e istituzione. Lo Spirito interroga i religiosi*, Roma 1983, pp. 203–15. This year also the acceptance by Rome of the meetings of young people at Taizé, the monastery in Burgundy which has taken great care not to become a movement.

63. 'Il primo convegno di Roma (23–27 settembre 1981)' in M. Camisasca and M. Vitali (eds), *I movimenti nella chiesa degli anni '80, Atti del I convegno internazionale*, Milan 1982; there is a balanced view in the editorial 'I Movimenti nella chiesa oggi', *La Civiltà Cattolica* 132, 1981/3, pp. 417–28. The second meeting took place at Rocca di Papa on 28 February – 4 March 1987 and has been published as *I movimenti nella chiesa. Atti del II Colloquio internazionale, 'Vocazione e missione dei laici nella Chiesa oggi'*, Milan 1987; the third meeting took place in Bratislava from 1–4 April 1991. The congress of Pentecost 1998 replaced the fourth meeting.

64. P. Vanzan, 'Le grandi linee del dibattito sinodale sui laici nella Chiesa e nel mondo', in *La Civiltà Cattolica* 138, 1987/1, pp. 40–50.

65. M. W. Cuneo, *The Smoke of Satan. Conservative and Traditionalist Dissent in Contemporary America*, New York and Oxford 1997; on the agreement with the followers of Lefbvre cf. W. Dinges, 'Roman Catholic Traditionalism' in

Fundamentalism Observed, ed M. E. Marty and R. S. Appleby, Vol. 1, Chicago 1991, pp. 66–101.

66. *Das konsoziative Element in der Kirche. Akten des VI. Internationalen Kongresses für Kanonisches Recht. München 14.-19. September 1989* ed W. Aymans, K. T. Geringer and H. Schmitz, St Ottilien 1989; especially J. H. Provost, 'The Realization of Ecclesiastical Purposes through and in Associations of Secular Law', ibid., pp. 751–59; J. Miras, 'Carismas y estructuras activas: ¿un binomio necesario? Algunas reflexiones en torno a la institucionalización de los carismas', ibid., pp. 149–56; E. Corecco, 'Istituzione e carisma in riferimento alle strutture associative', ibid., pp. 79–98.

67. A journal of CL launched a harsh attack on Giuseppe Lazzati, ex-diocesan president of the AC of Milan and already rector of the Università Cattolica, recently dissolved, cf. D. Menozzi, *La chiesa cattolica e la secolarizzazione*, Turin 1993, pp. 232–63 and A. Parola. *Giuseppe Lazzati un laico nell'Italia repubblicana*, forthcoming. At present the topic of the quality of the movements has also been raised by the biographical account by Maria Del Carmen Tapia, *Beyond the Threshold. A Life in Opus Dei*, New York 1987, which describes the internal life of Opus Dei from the perspective of a former leader of the movement, and the similar book by Gordon Urquhart, *The Pope's Armada. Unlocking the Secrets of Mysterious and Powerful New Sects in the Church*, Amherst NY 1999.

68. [Pontifical Council for the Laity], *I movimenti nella chiesa. Atti del convegno mondiale dei movimenti ecclesiali, Roma 27–29 maggio 1998*, Città del Vaticano 1999, with the words of John Paul II to the 1998 Pentecost assembly, pp. 217–24. There is an apologetic reading in C. Hegge, *Il Vaticano II e i movimenti ecclesiali. Una ricezione carismatica*, Rome 2001.

69. For the debate see J. Hendriks, 'Consociationum fidelium approbatio et statuta', *Periodica* 73, 1984, pp. 173–90; L. Martínez Sistach, *Las asociasiones de fideles*, Barcelona ³1994, which incorporates the article on the competent ecclesiastical authority on supra-diocesan associations in *I diritti e i doveri del cristiano nella Chiesa e nella società* ed. E. Corecco et al., Milan 1981, pp. 595–610.

70. [Pontifical Council for the Laity], *I movimenti ecclesiali nella sollecitudine pastorale dei vescovi*, Rome 2000: it is interesting that in his *Dialogo*, pp. 227–28, Cardinal Ratzinger explains that the movements guarantee equal dignity, communion and reciprocal communication.

71. J. P. Chantin (ed), *Les marges du christianismes: 'sectes', dissidences, ésotérisme*, Paris 2001.

72. K. Lehmann, 'I nuovi movimenti ecclesiali: motivazioni e finalità' in *Il Regno-Documenti* 1, 1987, pp. 27–31; B. Secondin, *I nuovi protagonisti. Movimenti, associazioni, gruppi nella Chiesa*, Cinisello Balsamo 1991.

73. B. Zadra, *I movimenti ecclesiali e i loro statuti*, Rome 1997: there is a list of the statutes and recognitions on pp. 143–60; however, there is no analysis of the

circumscribed and symbolic statutory anomaly, still contested by Roman lawyers, which reserves for a woman the succession to Chiara Lubich in leading the work of Focolari.

74. On this topic note the reports commissioned by the parliaments of France (1995) and Belgium (1997).

The Jesus Movement

CLAUDIO GIANOTTO

The year 1977 saw the publication of Gerd Theissen's book *The Sociology of the Jesus Movement*,[1] which introduced to New Testament studies, hitherto dominated by the approach of the Bultmann school centred on the kerygma and an existentialist hermeneutics, a concept, namely that of the social movement, derived from a discipline, sociology, which to that point had not been regarded with much enthusiasm by biblical scholars, who were all convinced followers of historical criticism. It used this approach to interpret the public activity of Jesus during the last years of his life and the beginnings of Christianity.

I. The context: the third quest of the historical Jesus

At that time historical studies of Jesus were still dominated by the so-called 'new quest', inaugurated by E. Käsemann in 1953 with a lecture given to former members of the Marburg theological faculty, where Bultmann had taught until 1951. It was published the next year under the title 'The Problem of the Historical Jesus'.[2] In this lecture Käsemann, himself a former pupil of Bultmann, distanced himself from the position of his master who, from a historical point of view, had shown a radical scepticism about the possibility of writing a biography of Jesus. As a historian, Bultmann had maintained that this was quite irrelevant seeing that Christian faith, called into being by the Word, has no need to base itself on the earthly Jesus, presented and reconstructed historically; indeed it must dispense with this in order to preserve its purity and integrity. Käsemann's criticism of Bultmann was twofold. Theologically he emphasized how the christological kerygma itself maintains a strict link with the historical Jesus: the first Christians were interested in the earthly life of Jesus and the Gospels themselves postulate the identity of the Risen Christ with the pre-Easter Jesus. While it is true that it is impossible to write a biography of Jesus in the strict sense of the word, there is a need to be careful not to cut off the Christian faith from its historical roots and fall into a kind of docetism, in which Jesus Christ would be reduced to a pure symbol and the event of the cross would be robbed of its fundamental significance. On the strictly historical and exegetical level, contrary to the scepticism introduced by form criticism in the analysis of the Gospels and shared by Bultmann, Käsemann showed himself more optimistic about the possibility of rediscovering, in the documentation that has come down to us, at least some of the authentic sayings of Jesus which make it possible to reconstruct historically at least in broad outline the substance, if not the form, of the teaching and the main events of Jesus' earthly life.

Even if Käsemann's project in fact overturned Bultmann's positions, which at that time were dominant in the theological and exegetical culture of Europe, it remained profoundly influenced by problems of a theological kind. The need to find the christological kerygma in the preaching of the pre-Easter Jesus at least in essence or in an implicit form led to a concentration and orientation on demonstrating the continuity between Jesus the preacher and Jesus preached which Bultmann had resolutely denied. This was now found, maintaining the existentalist hermeneutical perspectives used by Bultmann himself, in the continuity between the understanding of the teaching of the earthly Jesus and that of the kerygma of the first Christian communities.[3] It is clear how an approach of this kind was orientated on considering the activity and teaching of Jesus within an essentially theological and religious horizon, and, in an obsession with eliminating the break between the historical Jesus and the kerygma which had been approved by Bultmann, inevitably ended up by shifting this break further back, between Jesus and the Judaism of his time. The priority accorded in this context to the criterion of *discontinuity* in identifying the sayings and authentic facts of the earthly life of Jesus led to an emphasis on the exceptional character and uniqueness of his person and the singularity and absolute newness of his teaching, which thus came to be isolated and uprooted from their historical and social context. This was in order to endorse that ideal continuity in understanding existence which made it possible to connect the earthly Jesus and his teaching with the faith and kerygma of the primitive community. It is clear that in the typical studies of Jesus made in the 'new quest' there was thus no room for considerations of either a sociological kind or even of a more strictly historical kind.

So it can be understood how the publication of a volume like Theissen's troubled the waters of historical and exegetical research into Jesus and the origins of Christianity which otherwise were calm and perhaps even a bit stagnant, leading to reflection on the new perspectives that this type of approach opened up and the possibility of putting the historical problem of Jesus on a new basis and examining it with different tools. In fact Theissen's book was accompanied from the 1970s and even more in successive decades by a whole series of essays and studies on the problem; this inaugurated a new phase of historical research into Jesus, the so-called 'third quest'. The 'third quest' was characterized mainly by a concern to describe the historical figure of Jesus within Judaism and the historical and social environment in which he was active by broadening the historical and documentary basis of research (going beyond the too narrow confines of the literary sources and, within them, of the canonical writings), and by adopting new methods of approaching the problem and analysing the sources shared by the human sciences, in particular sociology and anthropology. It was within this new context that new studies on the Jesus movement were made and developed; Theissen's book, quoted at the beginning of this article, is one of the most significant examples of them, not least because in its very title it contains the term 'Jesus movement'.

II. The origins of the sociological analysis of the Jesus movement

In fact the sociological perspective became part of the study of Christian origins at the beginning of the twentieth century. K. Kautsky's *Der Ursprung des Christentums. Eine historische Untersuchung* (1908) is an important point of reference.[4] Kautsky had been trained in the school of scientific evolutionism in the second half of the nineteenth century, adhering enthusiastically to Darwinism in its various social applications; he then began to make a serious study of Karl Marx's *Das Kapital*, becoming the most important ideologist of German Social Democracy in the two decades preceding the Great War. He looked at the origins of Christianity with the eyes of a militant in the struggle of the modern proletariat and analysed the phenomenon on the basis of the materialistic conception of history which was an element in Marxist theory. He defined primitive Christianity as 'a movement of unpropertied people of various kinds who can be brought together under the name of proletarians'.[5] This class character would be attested by various elements: the hatred of the poor and the oppressed to which in particular the Gospel of Luke and the Letter of James bear witness; the first sharing of possessions; the contempt for work understood as an instrument of oppression; and the constitution of a community which, along the lines of the Essene community, involved the destruction of marriage and the family bond. Kautsky repeatedly emphasized the organizational strength of the earliest Christian communism. The strength of Jesus himself is said to have been his capacity for organizing, and the very cohesion of the earliest community would explain certain beliefs, like that in the resurrection of the founder. The proclamation of the resurrection of Jesus after his crucifixion led to his identification with the Messiah attested by the Jewish proletariat; however, this was a denationalized messiah who was presented as a kind of universal redeemer, capable of responding to the need to redeem all oppressed people. Thus the movement very quickly succeeded in going beyond the confines of Palestine and also found a welcome in the proletarian strata of the pagan world. After the fall of Jerusalem at the end of the rebellion against Rome in 66–70, Christianity progressively lost the character of a proletarian and communist movement, opening itself up to the rich and educated classes and ultimately becoming a spiritual and clerical religion.[6]

Thus we already find the application of the term 'movement' to Christianity at the beginning of the twentieth century. This is not surprising, since it was from the second half of the nineteenth century that the term 'social movement' came into use to indicate a form of collective behaviour aimed at modifying or transforming the existing social order in a more or less radical way, on the basis of a specific ideology and with the use of some form of organization,[7] and obviously such an expression was applied in the first place to the new workers' movement. Once it had entered into common use, the terminology could then also find useful applications in the analysis of religious phenomena.

The year 1908 also saw the publication of another volume, A. Deissmann's *Light from the Ancient East*.[8] The German scholar had tried on the basis of a study of the language of the New Testament writings to establish the social class to which the first Christians belonged. The undeniable similarity that the language of the New Testament presented to that of the inscriptions papyri, and ostraca from the contemporary Graeco-Roman world which had come to light above all in Egypt, thanks to the researches and excavations of two tireless archaeologists, B. P. Grenfell and A. S. Hunt, at the end of the nineteenth century, suggested that the two complexes of documents reflected a common social environment which, as the non-literary texts suggest, had to be that of country folk and workers, soldiers and slaves, people who were for the most part ordinary and uneducated. The conclusion was that the New Testament had not been composed in a special language, as the divinely inspired nature of the writings could have suggested, or even in a cultured language, that of the literary writings, but in the popular and spoken language of the time, predominantly used in the every-day communications of simple and uneducated people of lowly social status. Thus the first Christians came predominantly from the middle and lower classes of society; they were opposed to the 'high' culture of antiquity as a movement of the lower classes. Here Deissmann arrived at similar conclusions to Kautzsky, seeing the first Christians as representatives of the lower social classes, though he differed from him in emphasizing the decidedly religious character of the Christian movement over against Kautzsky's emphasis on the class conflict between slaves and masters.

On the other side of the Atlantic, the same period saw the appearance of the works of S. J. Case, of the 'Chicago School',[9] in particular *The Evolution of Early Christianity* (1914) and *The Social Origins of Christianity* (1923).[10] Case criticized the theologians of his time, particularly the Protestant theologians, for absolutizing the proto-Christian writings, and above all the Bible, taking them out of their respective social and historical contexts. To this approach, typical above all of German academic and university circles, Case opposed the socio-historical approach, which gave priority to the environment and the society that had produced such writings. And he explained the ideas, the values and the actions of the first Christians as so many responses to clear 'needs' of the society of the time.

In reality, however, the use of the methods and the instruments of the social sciences in biblical exegesis evoked hardly any interest for the first three-quarters of the twentieth century. Exegetes remained interested above all in the literary and formal dimensions of the texts and their theological content; moreover the dominant hermeneutic, of an existentialist and individualistic kind, left little room for social problems. But the main obstacle was probably a basic fear of reductionism, i.e. of the tendency of the sociological approach to reduce religious facts to pure social phenomena, emptying them of their specific features and significance. It was this widespread fear, combined with the scant familiarity that theologians had with the social sciences, that kept these at the periphery of exegetical investigation.

III. More recent developments

It is not until the beginning of the 1970s that a significant change of course becomes evident. And in this new context the suspicions and accusations of reductionism were turned back against the more traditionalist theologians and exegetes, who, emphasizing the manifest intentions of the texts and their literary dimensions, ignored the whole process of their production, which had clear social implications.[11] An article by R. Scroggs appeared in 1975 which presented the primitive Christian community as a sectarian movement.[12] The author begins from those elements which, according to the sociologists, make a group a true religious sect and found them in the first Christian communities and also in the group of followers of Jesus during his earthly ministry.

1. The requirements of a sect

The first requisite of a sect is *protest*: in the unstable social situation of first-century Palestine under Roman domination, characterized by conflict, this is expressed by starting from the knowledge that God welcomes in particular the excluded and the marginalized. The second requisite is the *rejection of the status quo*, which is expressed in separation from the family, in critical violence against the rich and riches, in polemic against the class leaders, represented by the scribes, the Pharisees and above all the priests. The third requisite is *egalitarianism*, documented in a great many passages of the New Testament:[13] Christians consider themselves all as brothers, and the social status that they had before entering the Christian community no longer has any value; becoming a Christian involves a redefinition of social status. The fourth requisite is the *love and welcome* which Christians find within the new social group and which, in some cases, remedies a condition of marginalization in wider society. The fifth requisite is the *voluntary* character of membership of the new religious group, as distinct from other forms of religious belonging predominantly based on ethnic criteria. The sixth requisite is that of the *total and exclusive* character of the commitment required of members of the Christian group, which does not allow multiple allegiances. And finally, the seventh requisite is that of the expectation of a *better future* which in Christianity manifests itself in the eschatological tension with the kingdom of God, the coming of which is imminent. This analysis explains on the one hand the relationships of opposition and rejection which the earliest Christianity had with the society in which it was set and on the other the characteristic links which formed a bond among members of the Christian group.

2. A millenarian movement

1975 also saw the appearance of J. G. Gager's *Kingdom and Community*, an analysis of the social forces which modelled Christianity and accompanied its growth from the beginnings up to its triumph under Constantine. Using various models taken from sociological research (in particular the theories of P. Worsley and K. Burridge), Gager presented earliest Christianity as a millennarian movement, composed of socially disadvantaged persons who longed for redemption. But unlike the other millennarian movements, Christianity succeeded in defying the centuries and establishing itself as an institutionalized religion. How is this anomaly to be explained? Gager resorts to the sociological concept of cognitive dissonance, which is the situation produced by the frustration of the typical expectations of the millenarian movements following their progressive postponement in time and their failure to materialize. According to Gager, Jesus' death on the cross itself will have produced a sense of cognitive dissonance, in that it put his messianic claims in question. Moreover the expectation of his imminent coming and the end and transformation of the world connected with it was also soon to be disappointed, in that the facts made it necessary to postpone the date of the parousia indefinitely. Christianity reacted to this situation by engaging in mission and this, by shifting attention to new centres of interest, made it possible to overcome the frustration following on the disappointment of the eschatological expectations. According to Gager, the intense missionary activity and the necessity to consolidate the group in situations of difficulty by the legitimation of power and the control of forms of internal deviation help to explain the relatively rapid success of Christianity within the Graeco-Roman world up to its triumph in the age of Constantine.

3. Itinerant charismatics

Theissen entered this area of study with an article in 1973.[14] In it the tradition of the sayings of Jesus was studied for the first time from the perspective of the sociology of literature, which analysed the relationship between the texts and socially conditioned human behaviour. Theissen focussed attention on those who handed down the sayings of Jesus, and the relationship between their social behaviour on the one hand and the content of their teaching on the other. His conclusion was that the radical teaching of Jesus on separation from the family and a life of renouncing possessions and riches represented an ethos which the followers of Jesus embodied and practised. This ethos was not a utopian and unattainable ideal, as exegetes had often argued, but rather the way of life of itinerant charismatics who lived on the margins of Palestinian society. Theissen's theory inevitably caused something of a stir in the world of academic exegesis: now the radical demands of the ethic of Jesus could no longer be examined in isolation from the material and social conditions of his time or the social environment and specific interests of his followers. The traditional method of analysing the texts, historical criticism, was now joined by a rigorous sociological perspective which shed new life on their meanings and their scope.[15]

The Sociology of the Jesus Movement (*The First Followers of Jesus*) appeared two years later. In it the author set out to study the Jesus movement from a sociological perspective. The choice of title already indicated a first result of the investigation, which demonstrated the character of the movement of the group of followers of Jesus. The study follows a scheme which comprises three stages: an analysis of roles, an analysis of factors and an analysis of function. The first stage studies the typical social behaviour of the followers of Jesus. Here Theissen takes up the theme of the itinerant charismatics, whose radicalism, characterized by a lack of fixed abode and family, the rejection of property, the renunciation of any law and the lack of any self-protection, represents one of the typical forms of conduct of the first followers of Jesus. In a relationship of complementarity with these itinerant charismatics, within the Jesus movement there must have been sedentary groups of sympathizers, whose behaviour, necessarily less radical, was open and made more or less extensive compromises with the surrounding environment. Thus a differentiated ethos characterized these two social forms of the Jesus movement. The ideological element, which allowed the cohesion of the movement, was the reference to the figure of Jesus as revealer, exemplified under the title Son of man. The second element, the analysis of factors, studied the influence of society on the Jesus movement. Socio-economic, socio-ecological, socio-political and socio-cultural elements are taken into consideration. This analysis demonstrates how the Jesus movement developed within a society, that of Jewish Palestine, characterized by a situation of profound crisis and grave conflicts. Confronted with this crisis and these conflicts, the Jesus movement worked out its own response, which is the object of the final stage: the analysis of function. The functional project of the Jesus movement was to promote and live out, within a society in profound crisis, shaken by the weight of tensions and enormous pressures, a new fabric of relations marked by love and reconciliation, a symbolic representation of Jesus' commandment to love one's enemy. This was to be realized mainly through a constant éffort to hold back aggression, which could be converted, displaced, internalized, transformed or symbolized. As a renewal movement within Judaism, the Jesus movement failed in its project; but within the Hellenistic Roman world it gained its objectives, though it also had to accept profound changes and transformations.

4. Reforms of the structures of power

The expression 'Jesus movement' can have two meanings. The studies mentioned so far have understood it as a movement which was in some way inspired by or derived from Jesus: here the main (but not exclusive) emphasis is on the activity of the movement after the death of the founder, at the dawn of Christianity. But other scholars have directed their interest and their investigation to the movement inspired by Jesus during his public life. According to R. A. Horsley,[16] Jesus was a radical social reformer who set out to transform the life of the villages of Galilee through a reform of the structures of power. Jesus is said to have been decisively opposed to the structures of power operating in the family (he challenged the patriarchal family structure) and society (he challenged the system of exploitation practised either directly or through a local clientèle of the Roman empire). He is said to have tried to introduce the changes which he hoped for in society not by founding an alternative community but through a reform of existing society. His project was the construction of a radically egalitarian society, completely free of any form of hierarchy. It made a clear distinction between the oracular prophets, whose message also lent itself to interpretation in an eschatological sense, and the prophets who were men of action, as had been the case for example with Elijah. Jesus classified himself among these last. For Jesus, the kingdom which was proclaimed was a political and social rather than a theological and religious construction; it was an immanent reality, and the tension which can be detected in his message of salvation was directed towards an intervention of God in history which would lead to a fulfilment of that transformation of society which had already been begun with his ministry, extending to the complete abolition of any form of repression.

In J. D. Crossan's 1991 reconstruction,[17] the activity of Jesus is considered as a response to the social situation in the rural world of Palestine at that time. Significantly broadening the documentary basis and applying the criteria of multiple attestation in a rather rigid way, Crossan concluded that Jesus' preaching of the kingdom is not to be understood in an eschatological apocalyptic sense but rather in an ethical sapiental sense, as a message of direct communion with God, which leaps over any institutional mediation: it is a message of brotherhood, of material and spiritual egalitarianism, expressed in symbolic form through healings and hospitality, the sharing of a common table. While emphasizing that the environment in which Jesus pursued his public activity was that of the rural Palestine of the time, Crossan emphasizes the parallelism between Jesus and the Cynic philosophers[18] and endorses the hypothesis of a Hellenistic influence. The final cause of the death of Jesus would then have to be attributed to the subversive potential of this message, which threatened the foundations of the monopoly of religious mediation exercised by the priesthood. The movement begun by Jesus would be continued after his execution by a new presentation of his message adapted to the new situation.

IV. Concluding observations

As we have seen, the interpretation of the public activity of Jesus in the last years of his life and that of the first groups which in some way claimed to originate with him as a movement after his violent execution arises from the introduction of the social sciences into the sphere of biblical studies. This made itself felt particularly intensely from the 1970s on. This circumstance has produced a new way of reading the texts which integrates other methods of critical reading that are already practised; in particular, in the perspective of the social sciences the text is analysed as an instrument of communication whose genres, content, messages and objectives are modelled by the forces at work within the social system and the historical context in which the text is produced and to which they constitute a specific response. Moreover, this approach has brought to the centre of attention some aspects, otherwise obscured, of the social and cultural environment in which Jesus, his followers and the first Christian groups operated, at the same time providing theoretical models for their interpretation. A number of features are brought to light, for example the interrelationship, within Palestinian society, of the sphere of politics and the family; the dynamics of Roman colonialism in Palestine (military occupation, taxation, the confiscation of lands, etc.) and its detrimental effects on the Jewish population; the main forms of social organization; the dominant institutions and models of behaviour; the models for forming parties and factions in competition with one another; the occasions for conflicts; roles and social stratification; the dominant cultural values and their relationships with the interests of the various groups; the construction of systems of alternative beliefs, traditions, rites, conceptions of the world and ideologies and the way in which they were spread by specific groups, and so on.[19] One of the consequences of the integration of these new perspectives into the study of the environment of Jesus and earliest Christianity is the need to rebalance the weight of different elements in the reconstruction of the complex framework: the action of Jesus and the first Christians was not just ideological (the transmission of ideas, however revolutionary they may have been), nor did it only follow channels of transmission from individual to individual (for example the master-disciple relationship), as scholars had tended to think, but it had an important impact on the society of the time and tried to transform it concretely in some way. There remains open the question of the specific features of a religious movement by comparison with movements of another type: on this scholars, while rejecting the forms of extreme reductionism evident at the beginning of the twentieth century, have different positions and feelings.

Translated by John Bowden

Notes

1. Gerd Theissen, *Soziologie der Jesusbewegung. Ein Beitrag zur Entstehungsgeschichte des Urchristentum*, Munich 1977; ET *The Sociology of the Jesus Movement* (American title), *The First Followers of Jesus* (English title), Philadelphia and London 1978.

2. *Zeitschrift für Theologie und Kirche*, 1954, pp. 125–53; ET in *Essays on New Testament Themes*, London 1964.

3. Cf. J. M. Robinson, *The New Quest of the Historical Jesus*, London 1959, expanded German edition *Kerygma und historischer Jesus*, Zürich ²1967, especially ch. 6, significantly entitled 'Understanding Existence in the Historical Jesus and in the Kerygma'.

4. K. Kautsky, *Der Ursprung des Christentums. Eine historische Untersuchung*, Stuttgart 1908.

5. Ibid., pp. vii–viii.

6. G. Barbaglio, 'Rassegna di studi di storia sociale e di ricerche di sociologia sullle origini cristiane I', *RivBiblIt* 36, 1988, p. 397.

7. Cf. L. Gallino, *Dizionario di sociologia*, Turin 1978, s.v. 'movimento sociale',. pp. 451–55.

8. A. Deissmann, *Light from the Ancient East*, London 1910.

9. For the Chicago school see R. W. Funk, 'The Watershed of the American Biblical Tradition: the Chicago School, First Phase, 1892–1920', *Journal of Biblical Literature* 95, 1976, pp. 4–22; W. J. Hynes, *Shirley Jackson Case and the Chicago School: The Socio-Historical Method*, Chico, CA 1981.

10. S. J. Case, *The Evolution of Early Christianity*, Chicago 1914; id., *The Social Origins of Christianity*, Chicago 1923.

11. See e.g. W.A. Meeks, *The First Urban Christians. The Social World of the Apostle Paul*, New Haven 1983. In the introduction he tackles precisely this problem, recognizing the reductionism of Kautzy and Case, but at the same time guarding against other types of reductionism.

12. R. Scroggs, 'The Earliest Christianity as Sectarian Movement' in J. Neusner (ed), *Christianity, Judaism and Other Graeco-Roman Cults*, Vol. II, Leiden 1975, pp. 1–23.

13. Cf. e.g. Gal. 3.28; I Cor. 12.13; Col. 3.11; Matt. 18; and the first chapters of Acts.

14. G. Theissen, 'Wanderradikalismus: literatursoziologische Aspekte der Über-lieferung von Worten Jesu im Urchristentum', *Zeitschrift für Theologie und Kirche* 70, 1973, pp. 245–71; now also in G. Theissen, *Studien zur Soziologie des Urchristentums*, Tübingen ²1983, pp. 79–105.

15. Cf. J. H. Elliott, *What Is Social-Scientific Criticism?*, Minneapolis 1993, pp. 17–35.

16. R. A. Horsley, *Jesus and the Spiral of Violence*, San Francisco 1987.

17. J. D. Crossan, *The Historical Jesus. The Life of a Mediterranean Jewish Peasant*, San Francisco 1991.

18. Cf. F. G. Downing, *Christ and the Cynics. Jesus and Other Radical Preachers in First Century Tradition*, Sheffield 1988.

19. Cf. Elliott, *What Is Social-Scientific Criticism?* (n. 15), pp. 32–34.

II. Historical Landscape

Pelagianism: From an Ethical Religious Movement to a Heresy and Back Again

MATHIJS LAMBERIGTS

Introduction

Traditional textbooks on the history of theology regularly contain an extensive discussion of the Pelagian heresy.[1] It is presented as a Western error dating from the fifth century which exaggerated the power of free will and rejected the doctrine of original sin and the need for grace.[2] In more recent patristic literature the tone is rather more moderate: it speaks of the Pelagian controversy. This is then regarded as the first theological controversy which took place predominantly among Christians from the Western part of the Roman empire,[3] and which in its reception has left deep traces on the history of Western theology. At least two parties are needed for a controversy to develop, and by far the most intelligent opponent of the Pelagians, Augustine of Hippo, gained the title *doctor gratiae* from the controversy precisely because he presented himself as a great defender of grace against the *inimici gratiae*, the 'enemies of grace'.[4] Augustine evidently succeeded in creating an often succinct picture of a coherent heterodox system of thought.[5] However, it is notable that the Christian tradition at the same time both supported Augustine's opposition to the Pelagians and thought it worth while preserving so-called Pelagian writings, if need be under the name of their opponents. The most striking example of this is beyond doubt Pelagius' *Epistula ad Demetriadem*, for which for a long time both Jerome and Augustine were presented as possible candidates for authorship,[6] because of the highly ascetic content of the work.

In this all too brief article I shall go back to the time before the open controversy between Augustine and the Pelagians. First I want to indicate the intuitions of Pelagius and the great resonance that they found in the West. Then by means of works written in Sicily I shall show how here we clearly have a broader current in the Western church. Finally I shall ask why this movement was ultimately regarded as 'heretical'.

I. A Christian movement

Because in 380 Christianity was elevated to the rank of a state religion, many people decided to convert to it, because such a conversion could markedly improve their career possibilities. Conversions contributed to the rapid growth of the church, and because of this rapid growth the church could not adequately continue to impose rigorous conditions on those being admitted to the Christian faith.

1. A truly Christian life

The lowering of the conditions for acceptance into the church not only led to its rapid growth, but also to the flourishing of monasticism, also in the West; it would find its way to Milan, for example, in the second half of the fourth century. Individuals, too, strove to take their Christian identity seriously. Pelagius was one of them. He was born in Britain and during the years 385–410 enjoyed a reputation in Rome as a Christian ascetic and teacher. In the Roman milieu, influenced by the Stoic ethic of virtues, Pelagius' plea for a lofty Christian life proved successful in the circles of the Christian aristocracy.[7] His ideas not only proved extremely attractive to younger figures like Caelestius, James, Timasius or Sixtus, later to become pope of Rome, but were also valued by Paulinus of Nola and (certainly before 415) Augustine. The milieu to which, for example, Melania and Pinianus belonged was appreciative of the one who argued earnestly for a return to a truly Christian life. Pelagius had found inspiration and support for his ideas in Ambrose, Jerome, whose success among aristocratic women is well known,[8] and the young Augustine. This plea for an authentic life was certainly not unique. Something similar also took place in Spain with Priscillian and in Gaul with Martin of Tours.[9] Moreover, in the circles which Pelagius frequented there was also great admiration for John Chrysostom, the 'moral theologian'; from the East. Chrysostom was to defend Aemilius of Beneventum, supposedly the father-in-law of Julian of Aeclanum, in the East on behalf of pope Innocent.[10] Precisely in this region (Campania and Apuleia) there were to be the fiercest protests by a group of nineteen bishops against the later condemnation of Pelagius. Pelagius himself clearly wanted to be a man of the church. In his commentaries on the letters of Paul he presented himself as an orthodox Christian. For this reason he was against Arianism, Manichaeism and also the positions of Jovinian.[11] Especially Pelagius' opposition to the second current explains why he put so much emphasis on the existence of free will: he regarded Manichaean determinism as a danger for a truly Christian ethic, which in his judgment was possible only in so far as elements like freedom and responsibility were guaranteed. Pelagius related true Christian life to the old adage that outside the church there is no salvation. Pelagius wanted to practise his Christians ideals as an ascetic *within* the church because he believed that only in the church as a mediating authority is salvation in Christ attained. That the holiness of the church as the body of Christ is essentially connected with the holiness of its members was taken for granted, but striving for holiness was closely bound up with the virtue of humility because of the recognition of one's own limitations.[12] Pelagius argued for authentic Christians, not for Novatian perfectionism.[13] But it was also clear to him that the grace of baptism also entailed ethical obligations and that the holiness of the church was a task for believers.[14]

His message struck home. This was evident for example in 413 when together with Innocent, Bishop of Rome, Augustine and Jerome he was asked to write a letter to Demetrias, the granddaughter of Proba (from the family of the Anicii, at that point one of the richest families in the empire). After Alaric's invasion in 410 the family had withdrawn to one of their estates in Africa. Demetrias could count on the support of Augustine and his friend Alypius of Thagaste for her religious upbringing. Like many women in this period the girl had decided not to marry but to take the veil. In his letter to Demetrias, Pelagius emphasized the goodness of human nature precisely because it is a gift of God, God, who gave human beings freedom to say yes or no to his offer of salvation (*Epistula ad Demetriadem* 2.2; 3.2). This goodness required Demetrias to act accordingly. The letter suggested ways of arriving at Christian perfection on the basis of an authentic Christian life. Christ's coming and gift of grace played a crucial role here (*Epistula ad Demetriadem* 8.4). Pelagius attached great importance to Demetrias' choice, which he described as a break with the 'worldly', earthly riches and the possibilities that they offered. There are admonitions to moderation in eating and drinking, an emphasis on purity, love of God and neighbour, and even of enemies, reading the scriptures, prayer,[15] simplicity, humility and also purity of heart, all well-known themes which we can also find in authors like Jerome, Ambrose or Augustine.[16] Pelagius himself appears in this document as a wise teacher, as a sympathetic person, and certainly not as a cold ascetic. Down to the present day the document has been called one of the 'jewels of Christian literature'.[17] The text was copied repeatedly in the course of the following centuries and regarded as a model for truly Christian life. This indicates that the writings were thought worthwhile preserving in the tradition.

2. *Radical commitment*

Parallel ideas to those of Pelagius in his letter to Demetrias have also been found in a text entitled *De vita christiana*.[18] Here too there is emphasis on the fact that to be called a Christian also meant that one was a Christian (*De vita christiana* 19). Similar views were found in an anonymous author who evidently had discovered the true faith in Sicily. In a letter to a young Christian who had been brought up on the classical literature, the author argues for a true Christianity, a total obedience to the law of Christ and a striving for true Christian authenticity, and again we find the idea that one is not a true Christian through words but through deeds (*Humanae referunt litterae* 3.1). Radical commitment is required of Christians, no half-measures (*Humanae referunt litterae* 3.2).

This concern for an upright Christian life does not seem to be limited to personal life. Evidently it also involves opposition to social injustice. In my view, the interesting thing here is that whereas in the official documents for and against Pelagians in one sense nothing can be found of their criticism of riches,[19] this point proves to play a much smaller role in Pelagius' authentic writings (cf. *Ad Demetriadem* 11); this criticism, which was predominantly to be expressed in Sicily, was to become the occasion for this kind of writing, too, to be condemned as Pelagian![20]

In 414/415, Hilary of Syracuse wrote in a letter to Augustine that around him were people who claimed that the rich who held on to their riches could not enter the kingdom of God even if they observed the commandments (but also kept their wealth). Hilary is referring here to the work *De divitiis*. A concern for poverty was certainly a topic in the Pelagian milieu. For example Julian of Aeclanum, Augustine's most intelligent opponent in the second Pelagian controversy, gave his possessions to the poor; for Gennadius this was sufficient reason to claim that he did this to win people over to his error (*De viris illustribus* 45 [46]).

3. Criticism of wealth

If we then take a look at the content of the *Corpus Caspari* (so called after the scholar who discovered the works which include the *De divitiis*), we can see that here we have a 'theology as knowledge relevant to practice'.[21] In other words, here is an author (and we do not know who he is, perhaps a Roman who lived in Sicily) who out of a deep faith in the good creator and his care for creation attributes to human beings the capacity to do what they have to do on the basis of God's gift of grace. Because human beings desire the worldly and engage in godless, irrational and unjust action, they do not what they can do. Therefore they need salvation from Christ. Christ's coming is described as an expression of God's will to redeem human beings from their sins and error through Christ and give them the right teaching and way of living through Christ. In line with what could be found in this period at the level of christology and soteriology, the author calls Christ Lord and Saviour.[22] He is certainly not primarily interested in theological views but in the practical and concrete relevance of Christ's dying and death for the men of his time. Because of what Christ has done, we need to follow him and become his disciples (*De divitiis* 9.6). The anonymous author is opposed to wealth. There is something attractive about his plea for poverty. His starting point is our natural equality and the fact that God himself wills that his creation should be accessible to all men and women (*De divitiis* 5.1–5.3). Everyone must have sufficient possessions, and no more than that. For the author Christ's poverty is the norm for our life. Christ's poverty was total, in other words it was quite concrete, and it was based on the conviction that God will provide in all things (*De divitiis* 5.3; 6.2; 10.1; 14). Thinking through the fact that we are all equal consistently proves to be the basic motif of a rejection of wealth. In his criticism of riches the author has in view people who at the beginning of the fifth century in Sicily were incredibly rich, while a large number of the poor there were living in inhuman situations. So according to the author wealth has to be shared. He argues that people must support one another in a Christian community.[23]

With his criticism of wealth the anonymous Roman put himself in an existing, moderate tradition. His writings also show clearly that this view of poverty is 'relative'. By 'relative' I mean that a large number of figures from the end of the fourth and beginning of the fifth century are praised in the literature for their choice of poverty, but at the same time prove to have the means of supporting religious communities. Melania, Pinianus and Albinus sold a large part of their possessions, but kept land in Sicily, Campania and Africa to support their religious communities. Paulinus of Nola is said to have been very poor, but nevertheless had the means to build. Demetrias gave away everything but still had sufficient capital to build a basilica at a later stage in life. The anonymous Roman who is an advocate of poverty was nevertheless in a position to issue publications and emphasizes that he found the way to full wisdom on the estate of a wise woman who had given up all her possessions. But the choice of these people, a number of whom had had contact with the ascetic Pelagius' circle of acquaintances, made an impression on society precisely because they put their possessions at the service of their neighbours. It was in fact a message which could find a hearing among the pagans. Did not Seneca say that no one can be worthy of God if he does not despise possessions?[24] Moreover, in the Gospel itself one could read that it was not easy for a rich man to attain heaven (Matt. 19.21–24). This made authentic Christian life concrete. It was a sign of compassion for the poor, a model of virtue and an expression of the struggle for perfection. At this level Christianity could join up perfectly with an attitude to life which was also popular among the pagans. There too one could find the decision to opt for asceticism because of the uncertainty of the time, the excessive quest for honour and the boundless ambition of others, themes which can also be found for example in Pelagius (*Ad Demetriadem* 6; 20.3; 29). However, we must not think that a great mass was involved. Moreover such a choice was not unproblematical: criticism could regularly be heard from other rich men who saw this as a form of religious fanaticism.[25]

II. From movement to heresy

The question arises why in a very short time this movement, which had broad points of contact with Western aristocracy, came to be regarded as heretical.

In the first place, this has to do with the role of Augustine. For Augustine, essential aspects of (African) theology were at stake like sin, original sin, the sinful desires, the central role of Christ as mediator between God and human beings, the primacy of grace over free will, God's omnipotence and the predestination which flows from it, to mention the most important of them. He saw these important elements put in danger by the Pelagians. In his reaction, not always correctly,[26] he brought the scattered views of opponents (not all of whom were real opponents) into a synthesis and then criticized them. Augustine thus also ensured that a very varied 'Pelagian' literature was brought together into a dogmatic system.[27] He went completely on to the offensive only after Pelagius' acquittal in Diospolis (415), where Eastern bishops seem to have had no problem with Pelagius' views. Diospolis and the reporting of it in Africa caused a shock and resulted in a condemnation of Pelagius and Caelestius at the synods of Carthage and Milev (416) and the confirmation of this by Innocent I in Rome (January 417). But even then one cannot escape the impression that there was still no 'monolithic' block opposed to Pelagius. Caelestius, who came to Rome in person, and Pelagius, who sent a letter and a *libellus fidei* to the new pope Zosimus, were both acquitted by the pope. The theological aspect of the matter had still not sufficiently been talked through in 418. But after the fall of Rome in 410 the emperor could not allow a new 'Donatist' controversy. Zosimus was compelled under pressure from both Africa and the emperor in Ravenna, to whom the Africans had gone for support, to condemn Caelestius and Pelagius.[28] Apart from a few fragments, the decree condemning them, *Epistula Tractoria*, sent to all bishops throughout the word,[29] has not been preserved.[30] It is interesting also to note that precisely in this period the emancipatory process of rich noblewomen associated with the ideal of virginity likewise came to an end. The time of theological freedom and spiritual experiments was over.

Conclusion

This survey makes it clear that at the end of the fourth and the beginning of the fifth century an important group of Christians from the nobility took their vocation seriously. This was a movement which argued for Christian responsibility, saw human freedom as a gift and a task and advocated an ascetic way of life, and did all this with one concern: to seek an authentic way of living out Christianity.

Until recently the writings of this widespread movement were generally referred to as Pelagian. The advantage of this was perhaps that the movement could be 'localized', but recent investigations show that we cannot identify this movement of personal and social renewal with a dogmatically coherent and 'heretical' whole. We could also find the ideas for which they stood among other, 'orthodox', thinkers. For example, *De divitiis* is no longer regarded as a piece of Pelagian polemic but as a 'typical text from that attempt, intensified generally from the Christian side at the end of the fourth and beginning of the fifth century, to provide a Christian ascetical basis of those attitudes, moods and mentalities which provide a support for and link with society and thus remould it in new forms of power and representation.'[31] The time was evidently not ripe to allow such an attempt. It is one of the achievements of research during the last century to have rediscovered these intuitions and to have relativized the Pelagian 'danger'.[32]

Translated by John Bowden

Notes

1. Good surveys are offered, in chronological order, by C. Garcia-Sanchez, *Pelagius and Christian Initiation: A Study in Historical Theology*, Washington 1978, pp. 9–103 (this concentrates on recent interpretations of Pelagius' views about the holiness of the church); F. G. Nuvolone, 'Pélage et Pélagianisme. I. Les écrivains' in *Dictionnaire de Spiritualité* 12, 2, 1986, pp. 2889–923; O. Wermelinger, 'Neuere Forschungskontroversen um Augustinus und Pelagius' in C. Mayer and K. H. Chelius (eds), *Internationales Symposion über den Stand der Augustinus-Forschung vom 12. bis 16. April 1987 im Schloss Rauischholzhausen der Justus-Liebig-Universität Giessen*, Würzburg 1989, pp. 189–217; G. Bonner, '*Pelagius/Pelagianischer Streit*', *TRE* 26, 1996, pp. 176–85; M. Lamberigts, 'Pélage: la réhabilitation d'un hérétique' in J. Pirotte and E. Louchez (eds), *Deux mille ans d'histoire de l'Eglise. Bilan et perspectives historiographiques*, *RHE* 95/3, 2000, pp. 97–111.

2. Cf. R. Hedde and É. Amann, '*Pélagianisme*' in *DThC* 12, 1: 'A major heresy which arose in the West at the beginning of the fifth century and, beginning from an exaggeration of the power of free will, ended up denying the need for divine grace, the transmission of original sin, the distinction between the natural and the supernatural order', a perfect reproduction of what one could find said by dogmatic theologians.

3. These Christians could live in the East, as for example Jerome did. However, the first opponent of the doctrine of original sin known by name, Rufinus the Syrian, comes from the East, cf. Nuvolone, 'Pélage et Pélagianisme' (n. 1), pp. 2890–1; cf. also W. Dunphy, 'Rufinus the Syrian's Books', *Augustinianum* 23, 1983, pp. 523–29.

4. There are good surveys e.g. in G. Bonner, 'Augustine and Pelagianism', *Augustinian Studies* 24, 1993, pp. 27–47 (reprinted in id., *Church and Faith in the Patristic Tradition. Augustine, Pelagianism, and Early Christian Northumbria*, Aldershot 1996).

5. In this connection see O. Wermelinger, *Rom und Pelagius*, Päpste und Papsttum 7, Stuttgart 1975, esp. pp. 278–82.

6. Cf. *PL* 30, pp. 15–45; *PL* 33, pp. 1099–120.

7. In this connection see especially P. Brown, *Religion and Society in the Age of Saint Augustine*, London 1972, pp. 183–226.

8. See e.g. C. Krumeich, *Hieronymus und die christlichen feminae clarissimae*, Bonn 1993; P. Laurence, *Jérôme et le nouveau modèle féminin*, Études augustiniennes 155, Paris 1997.

9. A. Solignac, *Pélage et Pélagianisme. II. Le mouvement et sa doctrine*, p. 2923, in fact explicitly speaks of a movement.

10. C. and L. Pietri (eds), *Prosopographie chrétienne du Bas-Empire. 2. Prosopographie de l'Italie chrétienne (313–604)*, Rome 1999, Vol. 1, A–K, s.v. Aemilius 1, pp. 4–35.

11. Cf. T. Bohlin, *Die Theologie des Pelagius und ihre Genesis*, Uppsala and Wiesbaden, 1957; cf. also G. Bonner, 'How Pelagian was Pelagius? An Examination of the Contentions of Torgny Bohlin', *Studia Patristica IX. Papers presented to the Fourth International Conference on Patristic Studies held at Christ Church, Oxford 1963*, Texte und Untersuchungen 94, Berlin 1966, 350–8 (reprint in id., *Church and Faith in the Patristic Tradition* [n. 4]); Greshake, *Gnade als konkrete Freiheit*, pp. 27ff.

12. See S. Thier, *Kirche bei Pelagius*, Patristische Texte und Studien 50, Berlin and New York, 1999.

13. Garcia-Sanchez, *Pelagius and Christian Initiation* (n. 1), pp. 104–16.

14. Ibid., pp. 161–70, esp. p. 169.

15. Prayer and the reading of scripture occupy a central place in this 'enemy of grace', cf. *Ad Demetriadem* 24.

16. Similar thoughts can also be found in e.g. *Ad Celantiam*.

17. Cf. B. Rees, *Pelagius. Life and Letters*, Woodbridge 1998, p. 34.

18. There is discussion as to whether Pelagius is the author of this text; but the interesting point is that despite all the hesitation over the authorship, one encounters the same concern for an authentic Christianity.

19. A. Kessler, *Reichtumskritik und Pelagianismus. Die pelagianische Diatribe de divitiis: Situierung, Lesetext, Übersetzung, Kommentar*, Paradosis. Beiträge zur Geschichte der altchristlichen Literatur und Theologie 43, Freiburg 1999, pp. 85–88.

20. Thus still Solignac, *Pélage* (n. 9), p. 2933.

21. Thus Kessler, *Reichtumskritik und Pelagianismus* (n.19), p. 146.

22. With his survey Kessler, ibid., pp. 162–63, again makes it clear that at the level of christology and soteriology one cannot indicate traces of heterodoxy either in Pelagius, or among Pelagians or in our author.

23. Ibid., pp. 194ff.

24. Seneca, *Letter* 18,12: '*Nemo alius est deo dignus quam qui opes contempsit*' (No one is worthy of God who does not despise riches).

25. Kessler, *Reichtumskritik und Pelagianismus* (n. 19), pp. 215–19.

26. See e.g. Wermelinger, 'Neuere Forschungskontroversen um Augustin und Pelagius' (n. 1), p. 202.

27. Ibid., p. 216.

28. Cf. M. Lamberigts, 'Augustine and Julian of Aeclanum on Zosimus', *Augustiniana* 42, 1992, pp. 311–30.

29. Cf. J. P. Burns, 'Augustine's Role in the Imperial Action against Pelagius', *JTS* 30, 1979, pp. 67–83. Cf. also Y.-M. Duval, 'Julien d'Éclane et Rufin d'Aquilée. Du Concile de Rimini à la répression pélagienne. L'intervention impériale en matière religieuse', *REA* 24, 1978, pp. 243–71.

30. Cf. O. Wermelinger, 'Das Pelagiusdossier in der Tractoria des Zosimus', *Freiburger Zeitschrift für Philosophie und Theologie* 26, 1979, pp. 336–68.

31. Kessler, *Reichtumskritik und Pelagianismus* (n. 19), p. 219.

32. Lamberigts, 'Pélage: la réhabilitation d'un hérétique' (n. 1), pp. 97–111.

Lay Religious Movements in the Middle Ages

ANDRÉ VAUCHEZ

Up to the last decades of the twelfth century, lay people who aspired to lead a religious life could hardly envisage any possibility other than entering monastic life or associating in some way with a religious community in order to benefit from the spiritual riches and merits accumulated in the shelter of the cloister by the servants of God. The forms of this association were extremely variable: the lay people who remained in the world most often contented themselves with making a pact of *fraternitas* with an abbey or collegial body, by virtue of which they were associated with the prayers (*consortes orationum*) of the monks or regular canons and with the benefits which could arise from them on a temporal and spiritual level. Sometimes family groups or peasant communities voluntarily put themselves under the protection of a monastery, though their members did not cease to go about their temporal affairs.

Some of the faithful went even further and put themselves at the service of a religious community as lay brothers, i.e. as manual workers who were part of an abbey or priory, where to a degree they shared in the life of the monks, but had a separate dormitory and refectory and were excluded from the choral office. Thus at the beginning of the thirteenth century a pious knight in the entourage of Philippe Auguste, Jean de Montmirail (died 1217), asked around the age of forty to be admitted as a lay brother into the Cistercians of Longpont; this was considered an act of great humility, since in general the lay brothers were recruited from the lowest levels of the peasantry. However, his case is not isolated, since shortly afterwards the seigneur Gobert d'Aspremont, having taken part in the crusade against the Albigensians in 1226, entered the *familia* (domestic life) of the Cistercian abbey of Villers, in Brabant, where he acquired a reputation for sanctity.

The crusades

However, one of the most distinctive features of the thirteenth century from the point of view of the history of spirituality is the appearance, among the laity, of an élite of men and women who sought to lead an authentically religious life without renouncing their state by associating with other lay people within the framework of a movement regulated by a rule. This phenomenon primarily involved the knightly aristocracy who, from around 1120/30 onwards, after the call from St Bernard, had seen a way of sanctification opened up to them in the framework of the military orders: Templars and Hospitallers, soon followed by the Teutonic Knights and numerous orders of the same kind which developed in Spain in the framework of the Reconquista. But these were still soldier monks, who as a rule had taken vows of celibacy, and their form of life did not appeal to many. Married rulers, like Ludwig IV of Thuringia, the husband of St Elizabeth of Hungary, who died on the way to the Holy Land in 1228, or even the holy King Louis, never belonged to an order of this kind. That did not prevent them from leading an intense religious life in the framework of the spirituality of the crusade. In fact there is too often a tendency to see the crusades only as military expeditions, a kind of holy war comparable to the Islamic *jihad*. This dimension certainly was not absent, but we must not lose sight of the fact that 'to take the cross' was anything but a simple rite: for the one who took the cross it implied the adoption, sometimes for years, of an ascetic and pious style of life which, before finally leading to fighting for the faith, for those who had made this choice and their spouses was represented by increased demands in the moral and religious sphere. This is well illustrated by the private and public behaviour of St Louis between 1248 and his death before Tunis in 1270.

Eremitism

Eremitism was another possible choice. Hermits or recluses were not all lay; some of them came from the ranks of the secular clergy, but the recluses, who existed both in the town and the country, were lay women, usually from modest backgrounds. The ecclesiastical hierarchy tried to group the hermits in communities and put pressure on them to adopt the forms of a monastic or canonical life. But above all in Mediterranean countries and the mountainous or wooded regions of north-west Europe, in the thirteenth century there were still many authentic solitaries who were held in great esteem by the populations among whom they lived because of their extreme asceticism and sometimes their power to perform miracles.

Brotherhoods

However, beyond doubt the most innovative aspect, which at that time spontaneously became the aspiration of certain lay circles for a religious life that went beyond the framework of the prescriptions made by the church, was the brotherhood movement. On the model of the priestly brotherhoods, which were then enjoying a hey-day, lay people grouped on a territorial – the village, the district – or social and professional – work – basis in order to practise mutual support and take charge of funerals and the posthumous destiny of their departed fellows. The communal dimension was in fact essential in these groups which, for example in Provence, significantly put themselves under the protection of the Holy Spirit. From one region to another, the way in which these groups were formed and their objectives varied considerably: some brotherhoods remained associated with monasteries or convents; others were more autonomous and called on priests or religious only to say mass or for occasional sermons. Common to all of them, however, was self-administration, and the majority – sometimes even uniquely – were composed of laity of both sexes, who voluntarily lived as brothers and sisters. In the thirteenth century, outside Italy the church hierarchy often looked with some displeasure on these spontaneous movements, over which they had no control and which they suspected of being hotbeds of anticlericalism or subversion, especially in the towns where the temporal power was exercised by a bishop or abbot. The clergy, for their part, sometimes felt challenged by these associations which were developing at the periphery of the parochial structures and becoming their rivals, by taking charge of the funeral rites of their dead members. So it is not surprising to find in the synodical statues like those of Bordeaux in 1255 a stern denunciation of the fact that 'the practice of the brotherhoods, which had been set up for pious works' was 'being abused by the malice of certain lay people who are making illicit statutes by which they are attempting to weaken the freedom of the church and to abolish the good and pious customs of the ancients'. And in Marseilles in the middle of the thirteenth century the brotherhood of the Holy Spirit gave rise to a commune which did not hesitate to oppose the power of the bishop.

The establishment of hospitallers and charitable bodies

On the other hand, the church authorities looked with a more favourable eye on the associations of lay people who put themselves at the service of 'Christ's poor', trying to alleviate the sufferings of the sick and to remedy the new forms of marginality which were developing at the time, from prostitution to leprosy. The result was an extraordinary flowering of initiatives throughout the West, which was translated into the foundation of numerous hospitallers and other charitable bodies. Some gave rise sooner or later to religious orders; others retained the form of brotherhoods or lay groups, like those which in the Rhône valley and in northern Italy committed themselves to building and maintaining bridges over the main rivers to facilitate the movement of travellers and pilgrims. It is difficult to tell precisely how many of these Maisons-Dieu, hospices or leprosaria there were. Most often they were founded by the local communities or by the middle class; in them the poor and the sick were welcomed and looked after by lay brothers and sisters, together with some canons or priests. But there seems no doubt that their number and importance were considerable in many regions of Christendom during the thirteenth century. In some markedly urbanized areas like the Low Countries and the Mediterranean countries, a large number of the faithful belonged to devout groups with the aim of enriching themselves mutually and progressing at a spiritual level. Marriage was the main obstacle for lay people adopting an authentically religious life: even between lawful married couples, in the eyes of the clergy the sexual act brought pollution, and virginity was considered to be the state of perfection *par excellence*. However, from the end of the twelfth century a development began in this sphere. Thus an important bull of 1175, addressed to the knights of the military order of St James of the Sword which had just been formed in Castille to promote the Reconquista there, asserted that the religious life was not bound to virginity but to obedience to a rule. Whether married or not, the knights who entered this order thus had every right to be considered as religious, to the degree that they had pronounced vows and put their life in danger in defence of the Christian faith. The importance of this text, which was confirmed by Innocent III in 1209, is considerable, to the degree that it shows an internalized conception of the 'flight from the world'. This in fact ceases to be necessarily identified with a rejection of carnal life and becomes a struggle against evil in all its forms, in which no category of Christians was a priori disqualified because of their way of life. The canonists drew consequences from this shift some decades later, as we can note in Hostiensis, who wrote in his *Summa aurea* (1253): 'In the broad sense, those are called religious who live a holy and religious life among themselves, not because they submit to a precise rule but by reasons of their life, which is harder and simpler than that of the other laity who live in a purely worldly fashion.'

Rural penitents

In fact, between the beginning of the twelfth century and the middle of the thirteenth we see the spontaneous budding of a whole series of forms of religious life for lay people of both sexes. This is the case with the rural penitent communities of northern Italy, for example, which grouped around a church or hospice to till the land, sharing their possessions and their work, having made a vow of penitence to a bishop or abbot. Even more original was the Third Order of the Humble of Lombardy, whose rule was approved by Innocent III in 1201. This group brought together lay people, married or single, who lived in the towns in their own houses in accordance with a 'plan of life' (*propositum*) which allowed them to combine work and family life with the practice of the ideal of the gospel. Very similar constitutions were granted by the same pope to the Poor Catholics – the old Waldensians who had returned to Orthodoxy – of Durand of Osca and to the Poor Lombards of Bernard Prim between 1208 and 1210.

Beguines

At the same time, in the regions extending from Flanders to Bavaria, passing through the diocese of Liège and Alsace, we can see those lay women called Beguines. Most often they lived in community, under the direction of one of their number, without pronouncing perpetual vows but combining manual work and help for the poor with a life of prayer. Among some of them, constant meditation on the sufferings of Christ ended up in a voluntary quest for suffering and the aspiration to total deprivation, as we can see in the case of Marie d'Oignies (died 1213), who is well known from the biography of her written in 1215 by her spiritual director Jacques de Vitry, future bishop of St John of Acre and cardinal. He obtained verbal approval for the way of life of the Beguines, but this was never confirmed by a solemn document.

Penitents and flagellants

In Italy, the most important groups of lay religious were the brotherhoods of penitents organized into an *Ordo de poenitentia*. Their existence is attested for the first time in a pontifical document in 1221, when Honorius III takes under his protection the penitents of Faenza, in Romagna, but beyond question they appear before 1215. The penitents' 'programme of life' (*propositum*), which in some respects is close to that of the Third Order of the Humble, took the form of a public promise of consecration to God. The voluntary penitents, men and women, committed themselves to wearing modest clothing: a garment of grey linen, not dyed, in one piece and of one colour. The simple fact of wearing this characteristic garment was the equivalent of a religious profession. Those who had donned it had to abstain from taking part in banquets, spectacles and dances, and to observe frequent fasts which were more rigorous than those of other laity. During these periods, married couples had to abstain from sexual relations, hence the name 'continent' which has sometimes been given to them; this must be interpreted in terms of a periodical continence, not a ban on sexual relations between couples. As for devotion, the penitents committed themselves to reciting the canonical hours each day, but the illiterate could replace each one of these by seven Paters and twelve at noon, to which were added the Creed and the Miserere at prime and at compline. They had to go to confession and communion at least three times a year (Christmas, Easter and Pentecost), and to meet once a month at the church indicated by their 'minister', i.e. the lay authorities of the brotherhood, to attend mass and hear an exhortation given by a religious who was instructed in the word of God. However, it is at the level of relations with the surrounding society that the lifestyle of the penitents was most original: the sisters and brothers were admitted into the community only when they had restored property dishonestly acquitted and renounced dishonest activities, if they had been engaging in them; moreover they refused to bear arms and to take oaths, out of faithfulness to the gospel precepts. In Italy this led to serious difficulties with the communal authorities. These incidents provoked frequent interventions in their favour from the bishops and the papacy; finally a compromise was found on the basis of a kind of 'civic service': the penitents without charge performed certain functions in the service of the community, from visiting prisons to supervising municipal finances.

In other contexts, the movement which led lay people to come together to achieve their salvation took a different orientation, under the influence of the eschatological conceptions of Joachim of Fiore, which were handed on and propagated in the Mediterranean regions by the Friars Minor. This was particularly the case with the flagellants, who appeared in Perugia in 1260, when a local penitent, Rainier Fasani, read to the inhabitants of the city a letter which he had received from the Madonna, ordering him to do public penance and to invite his compatriots to do the same in order to appease the anger of God. Terrified by the imminence of divine punishment, these latter responded to his call *en masse* and began by devoting themselves mutually to the discipline of expiatory processions. Flagellation allowed those who practised it to identify themselves with Christ by sharing in his sufferings. In doing this they were only taking over a penitential rite practised privately by monks, giving it a public and communitarian dimension. At the same time the faithful performed acts of conversion, becoming reconciled with their enemies and restoring goods wrongly acquired, in particular by the practice of lending at interest. The flagellant movement must not in fact be considered solely from the perspective of its severe physical or macabre features. When the 'Battuti' or 'Disciplinari', as they were called in Italy, met or went in procession from town to town, they sang spiritual songs in honour of God, the Virgin Mary and the saints while walking along flagellating themselves. And it is within their brotherhoods, when the movement had been channelled and institutionalized by the church, that a whole religious poetry and vernacular, hitherto without precedent, was to develop in Italy and Catalonia.

After the thirteenth century

The flourishing of very varied lay movements which characterizes the end of the twelfth century and the beginning of the thirteenth seems to slow down after 1300. It is not that the creation of brotherhoods becomes less common after this date, but that the growing control to which they were subjected by the clergy, both secular and regular, and the purely devotional orientation that the latter tried to impose on them, above all in the Mediterranean countries, seems to have made them less attractive. Under the influence of the spirituality of the mendicant orders, in fact we see a 'monasticizing of the laity', to use a phrase of Adolf von Harnack's, and the quest for a kind of religious mysticism tends to win out over the realism of charity and a sense of social and 'civic' values (peace, justice, care for the poor, etc.) which were at the heart of the penitential movement. Enrolled in the Franciscan Third Order from the time of the bull *Supra montem* promulgated by Nicholas IV in 1289, and thus obliged to renounce their autonomy and submit to the jurisdiction of the Friars Minor, numerous brotherhoods of penitents underwent a crisis at the end of the thirteenth or the beginning of the fourteenth century. In total, this tendency towards the 'regularization' of lay movements, accentuated by the condemnation of the Beguines and Beghards by the Council of Vienna (1311) and Pope John XXII, had disastrous consequences: many people then withdrew from these pious associations, whose purely devotional and female character continued to stand out. At the end of this process, the brotherhoods were led in the last centuries of the Middle Ages either to turn to prayer for the departed and mutual aid – as was the case for the vast majority – or to give priority to the quest for a spiritual union with God by mystical ways which could involve only a small élite.

Translated by John Bowden

The Great Adventure of the Catholic Movement in France in the Nineteenth and Twentieth Centuries

ÉMILE POULAT

In the Catholic Church, the transition through revolutionary violence (1789–1815) from the *Ancien Régime* to modern society led to the appearance of a radical newness, to such a degree that its opponents did not hesitate to speak of neo-Catholicism. There has always been movement in the church, as there has always been change. There have always been movements in the church, and always also changes. The great novelty came to be what under Leo XIII would be called the Catholic movement. We need to understand the specific nature of this new development, the reasons for it, what was at stake in it, its limits, its history and its significance for the present.

I. From the *Ancien Régime* to the Revolution

Under the *Ancien Régime* things had always been simple, very simple. To be a Christian was to belong to the church, which one entered by baptism, administered very soon after birth. The state was even more in a hurry: one was born a Christian simply by virtue of a declaration of birth in a Christian family and a Christian country.

1. From unity to dissociation

To be a Christian was to live in a world and a time structured by the church: parish life, the liturgical cycle, the festivals and seasons, the conduct of personal and family life, etc. It was to follow and imitate Christ (*sequela Christi, imitatio Christi*) through the commandments of God and the church, the sacraments, devotions. It was to live as far as possible in a state of grace by avoiding sin with a view to what mattered most, eternal salvation. The beyond and the world here below functioned in a closed circuit: the saints in paradise, the souls in purgatory, the cemetery around the church at the centre of the village, the communion of saints.

For the most pious and the most zealous who wanted to put the teachings of the gospel into practice, there was the consecrated life, monastic orders and religious congregations. And then there was a whole continuum to meet the aspirations of those who wanted more than parish life and less than the religious life. In a posthumous book which sums up his life's work, *L'église et le village*, Gabriel Le Bras gives a picture of what this old-style Catholicism could be, as does Jean de Viguerie in a more urban setting.[1]

The French Revolution destroyed this Christian social order, which was a public order based on the Catholic religion in France, but which elsewhere in Europe could just as well be Anglican, Lutheran or Orthodox. This destruction by violence provoked a reaction the two extreme forms of which were the Vendée war in the west and, in the diocese of Lyons, the missionary organization of a clandestine church by Abbé Linsolas, vicar-general of the archbishop in exile.[2]

Here we find ourselves at the start of a bifurcation, a divergence, the nature and scope of which historians still find difficult to grasp. It is a *crux politica* – typically French – which affects both the conduct of Catholics and the work of historians. Can we hope to get out of it?

The *Ancien Régime* was based on the union of the church and the monarchy, without confusing their roles: the church did not control the state and the state did not control the church, but they granted one another prerogatives and privileges. It was subtle, but simple. In attacking the church and the monarchy, the Revolution shattered for ever this simplicity and substituted for it a complexity which did not succeed in assuming the dualism to which we have become accustomed. The union was replaced by separation, indeed opposition, but the essential newness lies elsewhere.

In the first place, opposition to the Revolution was to be doubled: the service of the king and the monarchy, the service of the pope and the church. The distinction is clear from the beginning, even if for many people religion and the monarchy continued to be linked. This was to be the cause of interminable differentials, but there are two distinct causes: alongside the political counter-revolution, which has clearly been defined by historians, there is a Catholic counter-revolution the history of which has still to be written.[3]

Secondly, if the two causes are dissociated, and are not necessarily allied, what was to be the attitude of the Catholic Church to the Revolution and the society which emerged from it? Solitary and irreducable opposition, or a negotiated *rapprochement*? The question comes back. As Clemenceau said, 'the Revolution is a bloc', but at the political level it gave rise to several successive regimes – the Empire, the Restoration, the July Monarchy, the Second Republic, the Second Empire, the Third Republic – whose attitudes to the church and religion cannot be deduced directly from the great principles of the Revolution.

2. Steps towards a rally

The 1801 Concordat between Pius VII and Bonaparte can thus be interpreted as a first rallying of the church to the new order: moreover it provoked the opposition of the *Petite Église*. The Restoration did not reestablish the *Ancien Régime*: it was only a political restoration, and the Chambers did not grant the king an adjustment to the Concordat in favour of the church. Confronted with the religious indifferentism of successive regimes, the church did not associate itself with any of them and thus ended up in political indifferentism. The death of the Count of Chambord in 1883 without any direct descendant served the church by freeing his supporters from their allegiance to the legitimate prince.

All that seems to be crystal clear. But in fact an inextricable contradiction – a Gordian knot – indeed an inexpiable contradiction – took form within the church during the century. How was it possible to live without killing one another when there was manifest incompatibility in principle? How far was it possible to push the trial of strength, and at what point was it necessary to take the way of compromise, accommodation and conciliation (the term used by Pius XI) without reconciliation?

The first great step, in 1801, was the re-establishment of worship – parish life – at the cost of mutual concessions. The state took note of the religious actuality without subscribing to any religious truth and without attaching this actuality to any truth whatever. The church accepted this reduction without appropriating it or imprisoning itself in it. There was not 'the free church in the free state', to use the formula of Montalembert and Cavour, but rather the state in itself and the church in itself.

Other steps followed, beginning with the acceptance of the new legislation, despite unrelenting criticism of the Civil Code by the Catholic moralists and jurists. One example is the Falloux law (1850) on freedom of secondary teaching, to which the bishops attached much importance. The state was disposed to grant it in the framework of the great modern freedoms. Montalembert, who supported it, was accused of liberalism by

Veuillot, who demanded it in the name of the divine right of the church to teach, but he was disowned by Pius XI, despite his basic agreement with the director of *L'Univers*.

Right through the century the great problem was to be the diplomatic and pastoral difficulties caused by this irreducible disagreement, between liberals who blunted it and intransigents who exacerbated it. How was it possible to show oneself to be realistic without appearing to yield on principles? How was it possible to maintain principles without cutting oneself off from reality? This was not just a matter of prudent wisdom. Edouard Le Roy has written that in the church the faithful are like Chandeleur's sheep: 'one blesses them and shears them'. This was to fail to recognize that between the pastors and the flock entrusted to them there is a strongly structured public opinion of clergy and laity which has considerable means at its disposal. Leo XIII saw this when he involved French Catholics in rallying to the Republic. The church does not march in step, with finger and eye in rhythm. Obedience is a virtue inculcated from the catechism on, but it is also a domain unexplored academically for want of a thesis.

3. Counter-revolution

We must go back to the starting point: the Catholic counter-revolution. Today few are in a position to say who was involved in this and what it was about. Maurras' *Action française* cultivated the counter-revolutionary tradition. One of Maurras' Catholic disciples, Louis Dimier, wrote a book on the topic in 1917, *Les Maîtres de la Contre-révolution*. He mentioned thirteen of these masters: Maistre, Bonald, Rivarol, Balzac, Courrier, Sainte-Beuve, Taine, Renan, Fustel de Coulanges, Le Play, Proudhon, Goncourt and Veuillot. These were Catholic masters in their own way, not very Catholic or even notoriously anti-Catholic, with the exception of the last. Reading recent historians one finds other names which are even less Catholic. A whole piece of our religious history has disappeared or is being rediscovered in bits and pieces, as curiosities. However there was a powerful Catholic movement of resistance and opposition to revolutionary ideas which had no central direction, no leader, no national organization. The church was enough for it: it was the church, even if it was not the whole church, first of all because this had been crossed by different currents, and then above all because religious life was not reduced to this struggle.

The Revolution had created two words which Catholic ears found unbearable, 'de-Christianization' and 'de-priestification'. The church had lost its public status. It had seen a return of the time of the martyrs, 'in hatred of the faith'. It had seen a pope die in captivity, the papacy threatened with disappearance and erased from the map of the states. The Catholic counter-revolution was quite different from the political counter-revolution and not its religious form or variant. Pius VII showed this clearly by refusing to belong to the Holy Alliance of sovereigns which had restored his states to him. The Catholic counter-revolution preceded and prepared for Catholic intransigence and the Catholic movement which called for it.

J.-B. Duroselle wrote a thesis on 'The Beginnings of Social Catholicism in France from 1826 to 1870', which has not dated since its publication in 1951. He shows that what he applies this term to was not the prerogative of any family of thought within French Catholicism. One can detect a point here: the claim of a Catholic conservative made against 'social Catholics' who thought that they were the only legitimate heirs of this tradition. It is here that the confusion lies. The Catholic social movement which arose out of the directives of Leo XIII and in particular the encyclical *Rerum novarum* (1891) is not simply devotion to the cause of the disinherited, Christian generosity, a virtue of the heart, charity in action. It is primarily a thought, a doctrine which is the source of action, but an action the orientation of which is rigorously defined in advance.

This doctrine is focussed on three points: a critique of the liberal principles of present society; a rejection of the socialist way given the evils that it leads to; and the conception of a world to come – *ordo futurus rerum* – in accordance with Christian principles. Leo XIII was to mobilize all Catholic energies to realize this grandiose project, and in order to do so to try to discipline Catholic thought, which had burst apart into rival schools turned in on themselves. That was the significance of the restoration of Thomism which, for him, was not only a Thomism of teachers sensitive to its realism (*De ente et essentia*) over against the Kantian critique, but more broadly a political theology (*De regimine principi*) which takes up the problems of society.[4]

II. From counter-revolution to movement

From the defence of the pope and the church (*Pro Pontifece et Ecclesia*) and the activities of Catholic zeal in a hostile or indifferent society, we thus pass to a generalized offensive under the supreme authority of the Holy See. This could not ignore politics or diplomacy, but the politics was only a means or a stage: it was not the end or the objective. It was a matter not of returning to the *Ancien Régime* or of consolidating failing monarchies, but of remaking Christian society in new conditions. It is significant that the key encyclical, *Rerum novarum*, is dedicated to the question of the working classes, whereas Leo XIII did not write a single word on the rural question in a Europe 90% of which was populated by peasants.

1. Four questions

For half a century historians have done a good deal of work on the Catholic movement and neglected too much the Catholic counter-revolution which preceded it. Starting from what I have just sketched out, four major questions require reflection:

• How did the transition, by internal evolution, come about between counter-revolution and movement?
• In relation to the faith of the old days which was perpetuated by parochial life in a peaceful society, what is the new element in this organized opposition to a hostile society?
• In the end of the day – after two centuries and two great symbolic forms – how are we to sum up this gigantic enterprise – the great Catholic utopia – which left a profound mark on the church and stimulated its energies, but the goal of which seemed increasingly inaccessible? And what conclusion are we to draw from a spiritual success which ends in a historical failure?
• What is the relationship between this militant Catholicism which thinks that it is writing history and the ordinary Catholicism which populates the churches, too quickly reduced to its supposed 'conformism'?

   France was the epicentre of an earthquake which overturned the whole of Europe and of which the Treaty of Vienna in 1815 was the counter-revolutionary conclusion. Was the counter-revolution distinctive to France or can it be found elsewhere under specific forms? It is a constant of the Holy See, under Gregory XVI and under Pius XI. A recent European investigation has brought out from oblivion and obscurity 'The Black International',[5] from the capture of Rome and Italian unity to the death of Pius IX: unless this is thought to have emerged from nothing (*ex nihilo*), why not go back further?
   The Catholic counter-revolution can have many code names, perhaps as a strategy, or perhaps because it did not need this name. For us it is a convenient concept – like integralism or modernism – for bringing together a group of phenomena which did not necessarily live in the shade of or under

the sign of these labels. We must not forget that it had been preceded by the Catholic Counter-Reformation, and that for Catholic intransigence the genealogy of the Revolution begins with the Protestant Reformation and the humanist Renaissance (which is perceived of as 'pagan').

The Catholic Church lived in a state of legitimate possession. Everything was turned upside down when it found itself in a situation of opposition in which everything that it denounced and condemned was linked with the innovators. We have forgotten that in the 1891 encyclical *Res novae* is the Revolution. From this perspective it is worthwhile revisiting everything that shelters under the heading of Catholic anti-liberalism: an abandoned sphere, discredited authors who had a considerable audience. The whole of our religious history changes direction here.

2. Important persons

At the beginning of the Catholic counter-revolution we find people well known from elsewhere: Fr de Clorivière, the last French Jesuit to have pronounced his vows the very day that the pope dissolved the society and who would re-establish it in 1815; Fr Coudrin, founder of the missionary congregation of the Sacrés Coeurs de Picpus; Fr Chaminade, founder of the Society of Mary (the Marianists), the first Lamennais; and, among his disciples, Dom Guéranger, the restorer of Solesmes; what has been called the Congregation, with the Chevaliers de la Foi; the Brothers of St Vincent de Paul, founded by Léon Le Prévost; a whole flowering of works and movements the outlines of which I have sketched out elsewhere.[6]

This brings us to Mgr de Segur and the Union des oeuvres; to Mgr Gaume,[7] Mgr Fèvre, Fr Emmanuel d'Alzon, founder of the Assumptionists, who for a moment had the idea of a fourth vow, the vow of 'counter-revolution'; to Albert le Mun, pioneer of the second counter-revolution, the Social Catholic movement standing over against the Socialist Worker Movement: 'Socialism is the logical revolution and we are the irreconcilable counter-revolution. We have nothing in common, but between these two terms there is no longer any place for liberalism.'[8] Louis Veuillot said the same and thought the same.

3. A third front

We do not understand the history of the Catholic movement at all if we forget or hide its origins. It appeared, it developed and organized itself at the time when the socialist movement created a third front as an integral alternative to the confrontation between socialism and liberalism. It took a European dimension without imposing unity: every country followed its way, responded to its problems. It integrated the trade union movement and politics, not without major debates and painful splits. It was accused of 'social modernism'. It had to confront the problem of confessionalism and deconfessionalization.

In France the movement for popular liberation (which emerged from the JOC) and in Europe Christian Democracy must have believed for a moment that they had achieved their goal. But the fruits did not keep the promise of the flowers. The expected great clash between socialism and Catholicism ended up, contrary to all expectations, with the victory of liberalism and its 'modernity'. New ways were sought, mistrustful of any utopia, even a Catholic utopia – indeed above all a Catholic utopia.[9]

And there is more. The Catholic movement was structurally linked to Catholic Action and the great dream of Pius XI, the social kingship of Jesus Christ, Christ the king of the nations. These were then in close synergy with the action of the Holy See. Pius XI even defined Catholic Action as a participation of the hierarchy in the apostolate. Pius XII found the word excessive and spoke of co-operation. Catholic action then had all the preferences of the church, though these never found expression in its institutional structures. The 1917 Code of Canon Law maintains the traditional forms of piety and devotion; perhaps that was a bit early. The 1983 Code has tried to recognize the freedom of association of the faithful: it continues to ignore the specific character of Catholic Action. Might it be too late?

The Catholic movement and Catholic Action have ceased to be a model. No model has replaced them. However, we have not returned to the previous situation. It is a time of proliferation, but no reflection yet grasps the novelty of this situation, no tools for reflection have been put in place, no initiative has been taken, however much from all the evidence the solution has been sought. We are brought back to the basic recognition that Christian life precedes all reflection and that if communal reflection is indispensable, the vigour of this life depends little, if at all, on it.

Translated by John Bowden

Notes

1. Gabriel Le Bras, *L'église et le village*, Paris 1976; Jean de Viguerie, *Le catholicisme des Français dans l'ancienne France*, Paris 1988.

2. Jacques Linsolas, *L'Église clandestine de Lyon pendant la Révolution*, Lyons (2 vols: 1789–94 and 1794–99), 1985 and 1987.

3. This remark begins the dossier 'La contre-révolution catholique au XIXe siècle', *La Nef*, July/August 2002, pp. 19–29.

4. Pierre Thibault, *Savoir et pouvoir. Philosophie thomiste et politique cléricale au XIXe siècle*, Quebec 1972.

5. Emile Lamberts (ed), *The Black International. L'internationale noire (1870–1878)*, Louvain 2002.

6. 'Le petit et le grand monde des Ségur' in Émile Poulat et Jean-Pierre Laurent (eds), *L'Antimaçonnisme catholique*, Paris 1994, pp. 103–89.

7. Daniel Moulinet, *Les Classiques païens dans les collèges catholiques. Le combat de Mgr Gaume (1802–1879)*, Paris 1995.

8. Émile Poulat, *Église contre Bourgeoisie*, Tournai and Paris 1977, pp. 279–80. For L. Veuillot, see my contribution to Pierre Pierrard, *Louis Veuillot*, Paris 1998, pp. 211–56.

9. Jacques Palard, 'Les mutations du militantisme catholique en France. La dimension politique des ruptures institutionnelles', *Cahiers de l'Atelier*, July-September 2001, pp. 70–99; Ludovic Laloux, *Les étapes du renouvellement de l'apostolat des laïcs en France depuis le Concile Vatican II*, unpublished thesis of the University of Lille-III, 1999, summarized in 'L'apostolat des laïcs en France. D'une politique hexagonale aux impulsions romaines', *Nouvelle Revue théologique* 122, 2000, pp. 211–37.

III. Models and Differences

Increase and Multiply: From Organicism to a Plurality of Models in Contemporary Catholicism

ENZO PACE

Introduction

One of the unexpected effects of the theological reform introduced by the Second Vatican Council has been a move away from the principle which regulated the relationship between the institutional church and the various forms of lay gatherings and the participation of the laity in the internal life of the church. The transition from an organicistic view to the co-existence of models of organization differing greatly from one another lies at the heart of the argument that I want to present here. To put it another way, what changes is in fact the form of the organization itself, which is no longer grounded in the principle of religious work, based on differences of gender, age and profession, a form which had been thought to be a faithful reflection of the diverse expressions of civil society and of the personal and social dimensions of the life of the 'good Christian'.

The new development which made itself felt from Vatican II onwards is, however, the progressive acceptance by the ecclesiastical hierarchy of differentiation by charisms and functional specializations which overcome the traditional divisions characteristic of an organicistic model. In the organicisitic model, in fact, society is seen by the church (in its doctrine and ecclesial practice) as a living organism and naturally ordained by God, composed of intermediary bodies (from the family to local government bodies, from chambers of commerce to professional organizations, and so on) and of parts which form the natural morphology of society itself (the difference in gender and between generations, the different social stages of which the life-cycle is composed, the different degrees of instruction which the individuals reach, and finally, the membership of various social classes). Every segment of society thus represented constituted a peripheral cell which could be utilized to bring to life the organizational body of the Catholic Church.

Here we have a model of a corporate kind. Membership of the church was basically determined by the twofold criterion of belief on the one hand and shared socio-economic or natural bonds (age, sex, the generations, etc.) on the other. In this way the institutional church could structure society itself, forcing it to reflect all its characteristics and its internal features. It was not enough, for example, for the church of Pius XII to organize an association of Catholic doctors; it was also necessary to have a specific organization capable of bringing together Catholic obstetricians. Catholicity was at the same time a universal value and marker of the specific professional capacity of the social category that was organized 'under holy mother church': the sign that over and above the many differentiations characteristic of a modern society, the church was in a position to provide a sense of collective belonging (the symbolic benefit) and moral incentives individualized by professional category, age group and social corporations.

Here is another example: at a certain point it was no longer enough for the church after the Second World War to have supported the formation of trade unions clearly inspired by Catholicism; it had to organize its own internal association of Catholic workers which would be directly answerable to the ecclesiastical hierarchy, capable of the autonomous collective action characteristic of a modern trade union. Moreover, one of the largest lay organizations created by the church, Catholic Action, was structured internally by divisions and departments: of young people and adults, female and male, graduates and non-graduates, and so on. Every division had someone in charge (a priest along with a lay man or lay woman); for every department there was a specific methodology for handing on the religious message and a consistent application of this in keeping with the specific social situation in which any individual lived and worked. Hence the comprehensiveness of the system of action of the Catholic Church within society, the widespread sense of belonging, allegiance to its institutional aims, and the widespread conviction that there was an organic interpenetration of society and church: from the cradle to the grave in a continuum of individual and collective actions blessed, supported and guided by the church and its peripheral forms of organization.

All that no longer exists. That is not only because the theology of Vatican II has radically criticized the organicistic conception of the relationship between the church and the world, but also and above all because the model has not coped with the confrontation with a social environment that has brought about a profound transformation, differentiating spheres of social action and withdrawing them from the influence of religion. What has manifested itself to a certain point has been the reduction of the bond between universal and particular: the capacity of the former to shape the latter, in the minutest particulars and in the many specific social features which have characterized it, has progressively weakened. The nature of Catholicism has no longer appeared necessarily bound up with being a good doctor or a good scholar, an adult or a child, a graduate or an office or factory worker. Organizational culture, which was the inspiration for the organicist model, has gradually been volatilized. That is either because the faithful organized by corporations no longer seemed to feel to belong through groups determined by interests or socio-biological subdivisions, or because it was discovered that the unifying religious message could not offer light, meaning and direction to the concrete choices which each individual – as part of an age-group or social class – wanted to make autonomously, in his or her particular sphere of life. In the meantime the areas of meaning had become plural and relatively autonomous. The claim on the part of the church to unify them was no longer socially plausible, even among its faithful. It is no coincidence that all the big Catholic organizations have undergone a profound crisis, reflected by the weakness of the organizational culture which inspired them.

First of all I shall try to give a synthetic description of the new model which has come to be established over the last twenty years by trial and error, after a turbulent period of conflicts and crises inside and outside the Catholic world, and then try to describe the new organizational culture which animates it.

I. The plurality of models

What do Communion and Liberation,[1] Catholic Action, Renewal in the Spirit, the Neo-Cathecumenate Communities, the communities which listen to the Bible, Focolare and so on have in common? Their members are believers who live out membership of the Catholic Church in different ways. Being a member of one group is different from being a member of another, and not just for purely external reasons. This is because it affects the social environment in which a person lives, in contact with one association rather than another, or because one of these groups has a greater presence in one parish than another.

1. Social and religious environment

The motives of the various organizations are important: they have to do with a different conception of being Christian and feeling part of the Catholic Church. For the moment I shall put in parenthesis the history of the recognition of these new organizations by the ecclesiastical authorities, which in some cases has been laborious and complex. It is not the same thing to belong to Communion and Liberation as to undergo the route of reconversion offered by the Neo-Catechumenate movements. The boundaries between the different associations present today within the panorama of the church are quite clear and mark out considerable theological distances and forms of social and religious action. In the example I have just given, the faithful who take up the way of the Neo-Catechumenate movement choose to 'return to the origins of the Christian community', while those who adopt the ideals of Communion and Liberation try to reanimate spheres of social life, like the economy and politics, which have lost any Catholic stamp. In the same way, the followers of Renewal in the Spirit are sometimes perceived by the militants of Catholic Action as borderline persons who belong to a kind of free church within the wider Catholic Church. One could multiply cases and examples; what needs to be emphasized here is the complexity of the phenomenon. The fact that all the members of the various groups feel part of the church ('we are the church') does not mean that all express such a feeling in a homogeneous way: the diverse organizational structures in fact reflect a different theological view of the relationship between the church and the world, different style of liturgical life, diverse forms of the legitimation of leadership, lesser or greater declericalization of the principle of authority, and finally, relative independence from the ecclesiastical hierarchy both at the peripheral level (the parishes) and in relations with the church of Rome. All in all we have a high internal differentiation from the system of belief organized by the Catholic Church. It is as if the system had seen the growth within the social and religious environment in which it is set of a complexity which can no longer be reduced to the organicistic scheme which was so well attuned and praised in the past.

The theoretical presupposition from which I begin is that the social and religious environment has become much more complex in terms of systems of belief. It has produced a kind of religious inflation in the sphere which can no longer be controlled with traditional pastoral policies.[2] The religious question is orientated elsewhere and has become diversified in conformity to needs for meaning which could no longer be satisfied by the historical forms of a belief system

The history of the Catholic Pentecostal movement, which then became Renewal in the Spirit, is a good example. Born in the social setting of the United States, where the boundaries between Catholics and Protestants were blurred and in a phase of ecumenical effervescence, the movement originally presented itself as the interpreter of a need for immediate religion, critically in tension with the traditional sacral and ecclesiastical mediations ('the Spirit blows where it wills'), sought for not only in Catholic doctrine but also in the Protestant Pentecostal tradition and in the theology of the Spirit in the Orthodox Churches. In the same way, if we analyse the genesis of the Neo-Catechumenate movement, founded by two young ex-members of Catholic Action in Spain, then dominated by Franco, we can note that the inspiration arose from the need for a stronger and more radical religious offer than that traditionally represented by a lay organization like Catholic Action. The choice of returning to the origins of the Christian community and subjecting oneself to an intense and strict course of rediscovering the foundations of one's faith contains an implicit criticism of every form of religion acquired by birth. It is no longer enough for me to be born a Catholic; I feel the need to depart from the tradition. This is a post-traditionalist and in a sense post-Catholic choice, in the sense that it reveals the awareness of belonging to a society which continues to call itself Catholic but has not been for some time in the molecular patterns of individual and collective life.[3]

In the two cases I have just mentioned, the pressure to reform the world is very low; the problem is how to create the community outside the bounds of the institution. In other cases, however, the reform of the world plays a decisive strategic role. These involve new movements which, however, take up classical motives and themes either from Catholic integralism or social Catholicism, which arose in the second half of the nineteenth century. The reform of the world is in fact dear both to Communion and Liberation and to Opus Dei, and we find it with notable differences in all the Catholic voluntary associations engaged in compassionate activity within society. In the first instance (Communion and Liberation and Opus Dei) the works are seen as political and social investments aimed at recruiting, selecting and shaping the leading groups (from intermediate roles to the top levels of political command) in all those societies where they find space and recognition; in the second instance, however, the works are understood as a form of action in solidarity with a religious inspiration, capable of representing social classes which are economically disadvantaged or groups of individuals who are considered by society as marginal (the poorest of the poor, clandestine immigrants, human beings reduced to slavery and so on). In the former case an organizational logic functions which we can sum up in the formula of religion as a socio-political enterprise of the Catholic reconquest of the secularized word; in the latter it is an affirmation of the organizational principle of those who have no rights, the outcasts whom no trade union or political grouping is capable of representing and who stand outside the welfare apparatus. In this latter case we can use the term 'religion as a compassionate social undertaking'.

2. *Different ideal types of organization*

If we abandon case histories and try to identify the different ideal types of organization which can be encountered within a Catholic environment, the criteria to be used are:

- The 'spiritual life' proposed;
- The leadership structure and the division of powers and knowledge within the organization;
- The relationship between religious choice and active commitment in society and in the *polis* (directly or indirectly in political life);
- The attitude towards the virtue of obedience (to the authority of the church's magisterium).

The possible combinations of these four dimensions are theoretically not limitless, if we think of using them to bring order to a reality which presents itself as being very differentiated and, generally speaking, with latent conflicts which cannot easily be resolved.[4] If today these seem less visible and not represented in the public religious sphere, in the past the tensions between the various groups, movements and associations and their different positions have emerged clearly. The historical circumstance of the presence of a charismatic leader at the head of the church of Rome has hidden differences and conflicts, but without reducing the claim to 'count for more in the church' put forward by various Catholic groups with different theological and ecclesiological orientations, even if these differences are small. Indeed the competition has reached high levels when, as has happened, seeking internal legitimation some Catholic organizations have pointed to the sanctification of their founder to accredit themselves in a definitive way as 'pillars' of the institutional Catholic Church. That has happened recently, for example, with Opus Dei, which has succeeded in having its leader, Escrivà de Balaguer, canonized before the end of the current pontificate. This is a process of 'pillarization'[5] which others have followed in the past: many movements of religious reform which were originally lay or had little connection with the dominant pastoral policy at particular moments in history then became religious orders, thanks both to the power of their ideas or to the added value that the charisma with which they were founded succeeded in bringing to the universal church.[6]

To understand better what has just been said we can paraphrase the words of Carl Schmitt, in his study of 'Roman Catholicism and Political Form',[7] dedicated to the *complexio oppositorum* which is said to characterize the Church of Rome. Where an association or a group which has come into being on Catholic ground, within or on the periphery of the church, succeeds in translating the religious idea into activities (cultural, social, charitable, political, educational, etc.), it can aspire to be recognized by the magisterium and occupy a particular position in the scale of preferences which from time to time stabilize and mark out the relative nearness to or distance from the 'centre' of the decisions, where the directions of the external pastoral policies and of the internal organizational disciplines are spelt out. The church has an organizational culture which is by definition complex, precisely because its organizational know-how, accumulated over a history of two millennia, has taught it that it is 'there for all', including groups of believers who find themselves in different positions but also claim that they belong to the church. And in this case membership rather than belief is decisive in understanding the conflictual and plural way in which organizations inspired by different theological and ecclesiological models live together. To the degree that the conflict is not related to the principle of authority, tolerance is certain for groups, movements and associations which arise and reproduce themselves in time. The history of Catholic dissidence which has recently developed, starting with Vatican II, is a demonstration of what I have just said. When in fact the groups in dissent have put in question the 'virtue of obedience' they have been progressively expelled from the official church and marginalized.

3. *Two poles*

That having been said, if we practise the sociological *ars combinatoria* on the four dimensions listed above (spiritual life, leadership, attitude towards the world and obedience) and apply them to the morphology of the associations present in the Catholic world today, the ideal types that we can identify to provide orientation and bring order to reality are polarized in the following way:

• A spiritual model centred on conversion (the 'born again') and the re-founding of the community of the faithful; the predominantly lay characterization of leadership (and its declericalization), with the consequent development of models of organization which, alongside the canonical liturgies, favour liturgical forms of participation and performances that make transparent the 'communion of saints' on the way towards the spiritual rebirth of the Christianity of the first days; spiritual tension with the modern world, understood as a world where it is necessary to preach the gospel, to reconquer it for the spirit of the gospel, more and primarily in the consciences and not in the intuitions of the world; the virtue of obedience to the magisterium as doubt resolved either by the religious authority, which has ended up officially welcoming the movements of this type, or by the movements themselves, who have diluted the principle of obedience in the enthusiasm which brings about the awakening of the charisms at work in all the groups in question;

• A spiritual model of new identity, which expresses itself in the idea of the defence of Catholic identity (the defenders of God) threatened by modern individualism and ethical relativism; supreme guidance entrusted to the clergy, with a hierarchical organization which reproduces the classical divisions of religious work characteristic of the Catholic Church (clergy-laity, man-woman, intellectuals-ordinary people and so on); the world is to be reconquered, above all in all those spheres of life which have been withdrawn from the influence of Catholic thought (from economics to politics, from culture to the educational system, from the media to the sphere of love); obedience as a virtue is not put absolutely in question, because a public demonstration of it is considered by movements of this type as credentials for legitimating themselves and arriving at positions 'closer' to the heart of the institutional church.

Between these two poles we can find ideal types of intermediate Catholic organizations. These are the structured associations that we know from history or spontaneous associations that have formed more recently. All can be classified as complementary groups. In military jargon, the reserve officers are those who serve to complete and maintain the numerical and quantitative efficiency of an army. They are important, but they are not part of the active troops. In some circumstances they can become residual. To drop the metaphor, I might mention those groups with an ancient tradition (like Catholic Action) or of more recent formation (like Focolare or the groups of volunteers who head that real holding of social solidarity that Caritas has now become, whose complex model should be studied separately as an example of the innovation of the very culture of the organization in the Catholic sphere). Some of their features have been described; I identified them in the two previous ideal types but they are combined in different ways. In some groups, in fact, commitment *in the world* forms part of the universe of meaning that orientates the action of their members, but without turning this into the project of a Catholic reconquest of the world. The theology and ecclesiology of Vatican II seem to have been internalized; there is interest in being more committed to the world in the name of justice out of a conviction that by doing this the religious inspiration which inspires it will become transparent. Such commitment is far less to the project of building social pillars where the Catholic identity is in a position to give a visible mark to the action taken from time to time in the economic, political, cultural or educational spheres.

In the same way, other groups or movements are animated by a spiritual tension which is so strong that it forces them to present the spiritual model by which they are inspired in active life in very low profile; they are active in the world by assimilating to the laws which functionally regulate the different sub-systems of which modern society is composed. The model of informal organization, a net with a broad mesh, without real charismatic leaders and without any internal hierarchy, that we meet in Bible meditation groups (a large number of which have arisen and spread both within the parishes and outside them) or in groups of family spirituality (where the centre of the group is the family, which is thus outside institutional circuits but not against them) lead us to put this type of group in an area close to the first ideal type that I outlined above, without reproducing all its features. Neither the dimension of parallel liturgies nor interest in re-establishing the virtue of obedience through a revival of charisms are in fact present in the cases that I have just mentioned.

II. The socio-religious matrix of the plurality of models

What is the explanation of the multiplication of differing organizational models in an institution of salvation like the Catholic Church? It is not sufficient to note that the history of Catholicism is marked by cyclical movements which have progressively ended up by becoming institutionalized, perhaps after an initial phase of uncertainty and mistrust on the part of the church authorities. In fact Vatican II had unexpected long-term effects, and represents a real epistemological break in the organizational culture of the church in its complexity. Of course I am not speaking of the theological and liturgical changes introduced by the Council fathers. What is interesting is to observe how the manner of conceiving the existence of different forms of organization within the church has changed: for all the social and religious agents, the forms that they have created and inspired, up to those who perform the role of 'pastors' and representatives of sacred authority. The fact that it is no longer a problem for these latter today to recognize that there are different (and sometimes conflicting) forms of social and religious organization in the church can mean that something has happened in what Mary Douglas calls 'the thought of the institutions'.[8]

So is it possible to ask in particular how an institution of salvation thinks, by means of a secular capacity to regulate the symbolic conflict which develops within it in cycles, the internal differentiation which sees itself grow without having effectively promoted the growth? In such a case the institution of salvation is confronted with an organizational dilemma: is it to give up reducing to a unity the many and various movements within its social and religious environment, or is it to support the growth of the pluralism of forms of internal organization, because they are considered the necessary terminals through which to tune in to a social and religious environment which has become increasingly differentiated? In this latter case the acceptance of internal pluralism signifies that the system of (Catholic) belief seeks to transform the external complexity into internal complexity. No longer being able to curb it from above, according to the authority of the Codex, the Catholic Church limits itself to seeing whether minimal conditions of compatibility exist for a religious organization to be able to find space and citizenship within the church itself, without confronting directly the principle of the virtue of obedience.

Now the historical situation has been favourable to the development of many groups and religious movements with different vocations and bearing different specialized charisms, and on the other hand under the papacy of

Karol Wojtyla the power of religious authority has functioned predominantly as communication. It is as if the church of Rome, having apparently turned towards being governed by the centre, has understood that it had become impossible to control, as in the past, a social and religious background which in the meantime has become highly differentiated.[9] The history of many new religious movements which have come into being within the church after Vatican II shows how much effort the church authority has made to bring them into line; in the end they have been recognized as the expression of a religious revival which could not be catalogued and organized according to the traditional scheme of centre and periphery. Many of these movements are in reality self-centred (they have their leader, their own liturgies and theologies, different ways of understanding the relationship between clergy and laity, moved by a creative impulse which is ill-adapted to the traditional organizational routines).[10]

For example, the complex relationship which has been established between movements like the neo-Pentecostal, neo-catechumenal or neo-integralist (in the case of Communion and Liberation) movements on the one hand and the life of the parishes on the other illustrates what I have just said. In some cases considered as more or less desirable guests, in others providential for animating parishes at the limits of the organizational collapse, and in yet others internal sources of conflict between traditional parishes and 'new converts', for a great deal of their existence the movements in question have not known an easy life. Only recently have they been integrated into the system of functioning in parallel to the deregulation of the institutional religious space. In many cases (not only on the continents of Latin America or Africa, but also in Europe), the parishes have been transformed into polycentric structures, networks of different organizations which live together 'under the same roof' without a real reciprocal integration; consequently the parish is sometimes transformed into an offer of open spaces to offer hospitality to movements which can thus function, depending on the instances and the social environment in which they are active, either in a self-referential way or as a 'new leaven' that leads to the renewal of the life of the parish, clearly according to the distinctive spiritual impetus of the individual movements of which I am speaking. All in all this is an interchange between a system of institutionalized belief and an environment which has become highly differentiated.

Conclusion

As I have tried to demonstrate, the pluralism of the organizational models within the Catholic Church is an interesting case of paradigm change: from an organicistic conception to a systematic conception.[11] The various religious groups and movements present in the church in their diversity are not considered sources of potential disorder by the system of belief, but as a way in which the system itself functions. In modern societies a system of belief, in our case produced by an institution of salvation like the Catholic Church, must face the problem of the increase in its own systematic complexity. It is no longer enough to differentiate itself from other systems of belief; it must learn to cope organizationally with the differentiation which makes itself felt both outside (in the environment) and within. There are various possible ways of doing this: imposing the primacy of one form of organization on all the others which are virtually possible; introducing the principle of equal opportunities for all movements and organized groups tolerated in their relatively autonomous capacity in the production of religious meaning; or putting the various groups in a hierarchy in accordance with the criterion of their greater or lesser loyalty to the virtue of obedience. The thesis which I have tried to argue shows on the one hand that the first solution is now outdated and proves unproductive for the complex functioning of the socio-religious organization, whereas the other two opportunities constitute the two poles between which the decision-making processes characteristic of church authority oscillate, still uncertain today about favouring one over another.[12] But all that belongs to the *complexio oppositorum*.

Translated by John Bowden

Notes

1. S. Abruzzese, *Comunione e Liberazione*, Paris 1990.
2. N. Luhmann, *Funktion der Religion*, Frankfurt am Main 1977.
3. E. Pace, *Asceti e mistici in una società secolarizzata*, Venice 1983.
4. F. Garelli, 'Processi di differenziazione nel campo religioso', *Quaderni di Sociologia* 4, 1979, pp. 479–512; id., *Religione e Chiesa in Italia*, Bologna 1991.
5. K. Dobbelaere and M. Voisin, 'Sectes et nouveaux mouvements religieux en Belgique' in L. Voyé (ed), *La Belgique et ses Dieux*, Louvain-la-Neuve 1985, pp. 395–437 ; K. Dobbelaere, 'Secularization, Pillarization, Religious Involvement: Religious Change in the Low Countries' in T. Gannon (ed), *World Catholicism in Transition*, New York 1988, pp. 80–115.

6. J. Séguy, 'La protestation implicite: groupes et communautés charismatiques', *Archives de Sciences Sociales des Religion* 48/2, 1979, pp. 187–212 ; id., 'Pour une sociologie de l'ordre religieux', *Archives de Sciences Sociales des Religion* 57/1, 1984, pp. 55–68

7. C. Schmitt, *Römische Katholizismus und politische Form*, Munich 1925.

8. M. Douglas, *How Institutions Think*, Syracuse 1986.

9. J. Fulton, 'Modernity and Religious Change in Western Roman Catholicism: Two Contrasting Paradigms', *Social Compass* 44, 1997, pp. 115–29.

10. L. Diotallevi, *Religione, chiesa, modernizzazione: il caso italiano*, Rome 1999; id., 'Internal Competition in a National Religious Monopoly', *Sociology of Religion* 2, 2002, pp. 137–56.

11. N. Luhmann, *Soziale Systeme*, Frankfurt am Main 1984; E. Pace, 'Società complessa e religione' in D. Pizzuti (ed), *Sociologia della religione*, Rome 1985.

12. R. Stark, 'Catholic Context: Competition, Commitment and Innovation', *Review of Religious Research* 39, 1998, pp. 197–208.

The Ecclesiology of the Charismatic Communities and the Sects

ALEXANDRE GANOCZY

Catholic ecclesiology today sees itself challenged by the rapid spread of neo-religious groups which rightly or wrongly are called 'sects', often without any trouble being taken to define this term. The lack of theological clarity is just as great when, for example, renewal movements within the church which form significant minorities within the framework of the universal church are called 'Catholic sects'.

Questions and structures

Since the terms of the discussion are so imprecise, I want first to investigate the relevant texts of Vatican II to see whether they also offer approaches – in the framework of the evaluation of local churches and particular churches – to a theory of the small groups in the church which in the form of base communities or charismatic fellowships are increasingly claiming to be the church. A reflection on such approaches should make it possible to work out criteria for determining which new groups fully or at least partially correspond to the spirit of Christianity and which diverge from it in a decisive way. This can also clarify the question how, as the 'church from below', these relate structurally to the 'church from above' or, better, to the traditional institution of the church.

A second step will be to verify what has been worked out theoretically by means of concrete examples, more specifically by means of the French groups which developed after the Council and to a greater or lesser degree claim membership of the 'charismatic renewal movement'.

Since in the view of the expert analysts some developments in this scene show a tendency towards the formation of 'sects', it will be helpful also to attempt to clarify this term.

Finally I shall address some perspectives on the future in which the function of the new religious movements, Catholic and non-Catholic, in the development of Christianity will be discussed.

I. The ecclesiology of small groups after Vatican II

The Council showed great theological creativity when, while preserving a 'sacramental' and mystical ecclesiology of the universal church, it also attempted to focus on the existence of the particular or local church and in so doing evaluate theologically even the smallest manifestations of the church in groups and base communities. There is much to indicate that here the assembly of the churches sought to orientate itself on a primitive Christian, above all a Pauline, understanding of *ekklesia tou theou* ('church of God') that was a pluralistic one. In this way the Council spelt out its concern for *renovatio*, i.e. for the renewal of original structures of Christianity attested in the New Testament, though from the perspective of academic theology some gaps are also evident in its attempt.

1. The plural mode of existence of the church

This reflection begins with the diocese or episcopal church, which (in distinction from the *ecclesia universalis*, the 'universal church') is designated an *ecclesia particularis*, i.e. a 'particular churrch'.[1] The 'particular' character of these churches is soon also understood in an additive sense, as an element of a comprehensive whole (e.g. LG 13.3) or even as its *portio* (CD 11) On the other hand, however, it is interpreted in a representative sense according to which the particular church makes the whole church present in a real, as it were a sacramental-real, way. That can be read out of LG 23.3: the *ecclesiae particulares* (= 'particular churches') are structured 'after the model of the universal church', so that 'it is in these and formed out of them that the one and unique Catholic Church exists' (*existit*). For our topic, the formula 'exists in them' is decisive. It suggests a specific analogy with the local celebration of the eucharist: just as Christ is really present and exists sacramentally in this, so the church with its whole being is truly and actively there in the activities of a particular church. In this sense the relationship of the part to the whole goes beyond the quantitative and has qualitative significance. The principle of episcopal collegiality and its legal components can also very easily be derived from this.

2. *The local community*

The question remains whether this representative ecclesiality stands and falls by the fact that it is in fact led by a bishop. LG 26.1 seems to suggest an affirmative answer: 'This church of Christ is really present[2] in all legitimately organized groups of the faithful, which, in so far as they are united to their pastors, are also quite appropriately called churches (*ecclesiae*) in the New Testament.' The latter statement is backed up by examples from the Acts of the Apostles, where the components of office are in fact present.[3] But the Council could also have cited passages from Romans (16.5) or I Corinthians (16.19) about the 'house community' under the leadership of the married couple Prisca and Aquila: this is also called *ekklesia*, although it is manifestly not led by office holders. However, that does not exclude the possibility that the small group with the apostle and the pastors (presbyters?) referred to, which probably presided over the local church, consisting of several house communities and in it also over the eucharist, had constructive and organic connections within it. Paul does not hesitate to give such a group of 'lay people' the official title of *ekklesia*. This can be understood as an important beginning towards seeing these base communities, which arose spontaneously and had a charismatic structure, as representative of the church. That would also explain what the Council itself calls the Christian family 'as it were a house church' (*velut Ecclesia domestica*) (LG 11.2).[4] On this E. Lanne writes: 'Here there seems to be an authentic participation in the essence of the church, over and above any mere analogy.'[5] I would add that it is a participation which has a quasi-sacramental representativeness, since GS 48. 4 says that the Christian family is to 'show forth to all men Christ's living presence in the world and the authentic nature of the Church'.

Certainly we need to guard against confusing the house community (*ecclesia domestica*) of Vatican II with the *ekklesia* mentioned by Paul which assembles 'in houses'. But the two are structured in accordance with largely identical criteria of ecclesiality: the preaching of the gospel, fellowship through the Lord's Supper, the practice of brotherly and sisterly love, guidance by the Holy Spirit and the active presence of Christ. Preaching and the eucharist certainly call for ministers who have been appointed for this, even where these cannot yet emerge from the community and be 'ordained'. But it is impossible for Christ and the Holy Spirit to be absent. Their operative presence forms the absolute condition for being the church. They can also be sufficient where this is only coming into being, and only the basis is there.

There is much to suggest that the Council is interpreting Jesus' saying according to Matt. 18.20, 'Where two or three are gathered in my name, there am I in the midst of them', in Tertullian's sense: 'the church is truly there where people come together in the name of Christ'.[6] That is the case even when there are no persons in office as mediators. In fact Vatican II relates the logion to laity active in an apostolic way (AA 18.1), to faithful who act in the liturgy (SC 7.1), and even to gatherings of prayer with 'separated brethren' (UR 8.2).

Moreover the church assembly understands the local assembly or local community[7] largely in terms of a 'human locality',[8] i.e. not as a geographical fixation to a specific place but as the result of a concern for fellowship which is exercised here and now. So the church of God happens when people are baptized in the name of the Trinity, share the Lord's Supper (cf. I Cor. 11.18–20), express their own culture in the liturgy,[9] or co-ordinate their charismatic lay apostolate (AG 21). In such cases the Christian church occurs locally.

However, the representative ecclesiality which comes about in a human locality and often takes place in small groups is inconceivable for the Council without the ferment of the renewal which is constantly brought about by the Holy Spirit: the Spirit 'permits the church to keep the freshness of her youth. Constantly he renews her' (LG 4.1; cf. 9.3). Such renewal, which is made possible by grace,[10] lies in the logic of the Crucified One who has been raised as the 'new man'. All ecclesial groups are to participate in the 'newness of Jeus Christ',[11] though for them, too, the new life beyond death is only the object of eschatological hope. In the 'interim period' the Spirit of Christ works on all Christian communities with his 'gifts of grace' and makes them 'fit and ready to undertake various tasks and office for the renewal and building up of the church' (LG 12.2). According to this understanding, no charisma becomes merely individual edification, to guard a nest of pious warmth or for ecstatic prayer; it is given in advance for everyday achievements to the good of all. The charismatic renewal movements which have flourished since the Council have followed this understanding of charisma more or less closely.[12] I want to sketch this out to some degree, using the French communities as an example. In my view these communities serve very well as an illustration of the constants which can become crystallized in a particular cultural sphere despite the great variety of ecclesial modes of being.

II. 'Charismatic communities' in France

The great majority of the communities in question here understand themselves as 'charismatic communities' in the context of the charismatic renewal
of the 1970s. Their founders usually refer to an 'outpouring of the Spirit' or
a 'baptism in the Spirit' which they have experienced personally. However,
what this in fact consists of is seldom discussed explicitly. At all events it is
hardly connected explicitly with the Council's doctrine of charisms. This
tends to give the impression that the background to the phenomenon is the
North American Pentecostal movement as a theology of the gifts of grace
based on Paul, which is given to *all* believers 'for the use and upbuilding of
the community'.[13] Understood in this way, the charisms do not bring about
any transformations at a particular point but govern people's whole lives.
Consequently they are not to be understood 'in the sense of extraordinary
manifestations of the Spirit'[14] but as the capacity to pursue everyday goals.
For this reason (and with reference to LG 11), Yves Congar was 'reserved,
even critical, about the designation "charismatic movement"'.[15] In substance his view comes close to the definition by Heribert Mühlen that
charisma is 'a natural property and gift, in so far as it is released through the
Holy Spirit and is taken into service for the building up and growth' of
church and world.[16]

To this degree the scene of the French communities displays features
which incur the criticism sketched out here; do they even approach a 'sect'?
Or in general, do they too not display characteristics of the conciliar ecclesiology which correspond to the theology of renewal implied in it?

1. Sects or church communities?

As far as I can judge, these communities attach little value to a clear
definition of the term charism. What they understand by 'charismatic' can
be read more off their praxis. However, it is striking what importance here is
attached to strong personalities, men and women like Lanza del Vasto, Jean
Vanier, Roger Schutz, Sister Emmanuelle, Abbé Pierre, and others who are
less well known. Their example and their influence often create 'schools' and
attract a spontaneous following. In many cases such model figures found
their own community, in which their personal 'gift of grace' communicates
with identical or like-minded people. The founder becomes the 'leader', the
'pastor' ('*berger*'),[17] whose authority is decisive. At this point here and now –
often against the background of a heightened father image – a kind of per-

sonality cult develops[18] which can markedly hinder the free dialogue of charisms and create conditions like those surrounding a sect.[19] But this can be successfully avoided where there is a communal testing of the charisms and decisions on the Pauline model (cf. I Cor. 14.29–33). In that case authoritarianism gives way to mutual, as it were 'collegial', obedience; this can be observed particularly well in 'The New Way' (*Le Chemin Neuf*) community initiated by the Jesuits.[20]

To what do members feel called? To a form of common life arrived at by free decision and through the prayer of the group.[21] As in the primitive community in Jerusalem (cf. Acts 2.43–46), this nurtures the will to share both spiritual and material goods. There is a partial sharing of goods, e.g. to the extent of paying 10% of income into the community fund.[22] The way in which married couples with children live alongside unmarried lay people, women religious and clergy in an informal community,[23] sometimes in monasteries and convents which were formerly almost empty, is particularly characteristic of the scene.[24] These charismatics are marked by a particular love of children: often half of the community consists of small children.[25] Is the reason for this that in most cases the women remain fixed to the role of mother? That they are voluntarily restrained, understanding themselves as guardians of the inner life, and do not take on any responsibility for leadership?[26] Two-thirds of the 'Jacob's Well' (*Puits de Jacob*) community are women, but here too the real leadership lies in the hands of Jesuit fathers.[27] It is a great exception for a woman to be a 'pastor'.[28] At this point a real theological and anthropological lack can be noted in the French scene.

2. Bulwark against sectarianism

Well aware that an over-personalized understanding of charisms with a marked emphasis on feeling can bring them close to becoming sects, the communities never tire of claiming that they are indeed part of the church. Here, too, praxis prevails over any theory. I have found no trace of any reflection on the group as representative of the church along the lines of LG, but I have found a universal concern to be recognized by the hierarchy and to work together with the bishop of the local church,[29] to be given pastoral tasks by him[30] and to observe the pope's regulations closely. This loyalty led Paul VI in 1975 to call the 'charismatic renewal' an 'opportunity for the church and the world',[31] and John Paul II to praise its role in the 'new evangelization'.[32] This remark is in part to be read in the context of the fact that some communities, above all 'The New Way', have proved to be a breeding ground for priestly vocations. The desire for the ordination of married men (*viri probati*) makes itself felt more on the periphery.

The other dam against sectarian tendencies consists in the openness to the world and affirmation of the world which is present almost everywhere. Here charisma does not lose its reference to the world; it clearly comes close to the Pauline and conciliar idea and as a call also to renew social life in the spirit of the gospel. Here the French charismatics come very close to the Latin American base communities. They too want to contribute to the 'raising up and development' of the disadvantaged, albeit by other means.[33] Granted, they have not developed a 'theology of liberation', but in a similar way they are concerned to promote education, to care for the poor and homeless, and also to provide care for the handicapped, the victims of drugs, prisoners and pregnant women who do not know where to turn: 'Lion of Judah' (*Lion de Juda*) has succeeded in avoiding abortion in a good 30% of cases.[34] Granted, 'The New Way', which is particularly representative here, displays élitist features in so far as its ranks include many doctors, psychologists, teachers and intellectuals,[35] and it combines charism very closely with job,[36] but that does not exclude a marked social concern along the lines of papal social doctrine.

Practice also prevails over theory in ecumenical matters. Interconfessional theological dialogue does not stand in the foreground, but there is a marked concern to relativize the confessional boundaries in practice. Thus for example Reformed believers become members of Catholic communities,[37] and converted Protestant pastors join them,[38] which of course is not looked on with favour by their Protestant partners. But on the whole the spirit of Taizé tends to prevail. All in all, it seems to me to be the case that the notion of reform is understood and put forward in a positive, indeed optimistic, sense. The consciousness of bringing about church renewal by a personal return to the gospel and the original authenticity of the church of God, as a ferment of church renewal (which was also striven for by Vatican II), recalls both Francis of Assisi and Martin Luther. Thus here a priori the 'Reformation' element goes beyond confessional bounds.[39]

3. The interpretation of scripture

In this context it is also evident how far the spirituality striven for is orientated on biblical sources.[40] In the majority of cases, however, the interpretation of scripture does not follow the methods of critical exegesis – there are insufficient experts here. Rather, the faithful follow their own intuitions or the view of the 'pastor'. In extreme cases, of course, that can conjure up the danger of fundamentalism. But here, too, listening to the instructions of the episcopal and papal magisterium offers effective protection.

There is only very rarely systematic criticism of the hierarchy or protest against the way in which the institutional church acts. The communities want to be the church, both as the people of God and also as the organized followers of the apostolic ministry. Their basic assumption is that their own lay status corresponds to a call by the church, and realizes both the universal priesthood and the prophetic ministry of all the faithful in the world; this is largely in accord with the teaching of the Council. Among other things that means that the relationship between charisma and ordained ministry, or event and institution, is rarely experienced in terms of conflict. Rather, here too there is a quest for a complementary togetherness and collaboration. The classic parish congregations which are entrusted to the bishop in charge of a charismatic community are a good example of this.[41] Such synergy between the traditional structures and the new ones generally proves successful.

The reader of Monique Hébrards, the analyst of the scene whom I have consulted by way of an example, will be struck by the way in which the communities concerned take seriously the danger of coming close to becoming 'sects', at least in tendency (and more recent sources produce quite similar conclusions). For example, the charismatic group Emmanuel does not hesitate to practise street evangelization in the Latin Quarter of Paris like the Hare Krishna people and cry out to passers by: 'Hallelujah! The Lord loves you!' Those addressed react in amazement: 'Are these Catholic? We thought that they were a sect.' At the same time, however, this same group never wearies of referring to the statements of the pope. The fact that methods of prayer and preaching which resemble those of the sects are also practised elsewhere, and that they emanate a similar human warmth, is one reason why our groups regularly come into competition with non-religious groups, not least among the young.[42] But all in all it can be noted that the concern to be part of the church and to dissociate oneself clearly, but without violence, from the sectarian scene, can be detected everywhere.

III. An attempt at a phenomenological definition of a sect

What is a sect? The relevant lexica begin from the phenomenon of a group which has split away from a traditional religious community and rebels against it.[43] They then provide etymological information: the Latin name *secta* is not derived from *secare*, 'cut off', but from *sequi*, 'follow'. In fact it is evident from the history of religions that the splits designated in this way are almost always brought about by following a strong religious personality and observing his teachings. The key words 'school', 'party' or even – as in Paul (Gal. 1.6–12; 5.15) *hairesis* (i.e. 'heresy') refer to this process.

1. *Also outside Christianity*

All world religions have their sects, both in the past and in the present. This seems to be a law of the history of ideas. It should be noted that the mother community, above all the Christian community, does not necessarily and in every case radically repudiate such new groups, especially in the age of ecumenism. Its relationship to them is quite often marked by self-criticism, a concern for dialogue and practical collaboration, say, in the social sphere, and is sometimes marked by a kind of free competition (as I have just shown). There is a radical condemnation of 'sects' only where human rights and the dignity of the person are scorned; in this case state legislation also feels a responsibility.[44] In France in 2001, alongside the manipulatory manoeuvres of Scientology, in particular the *'Temple solaire'* ('Temple of the Sun'), which practices voluntary suicide, led to legal intervention.

These last examples confirm that the nature of the sect goes far beyond the specifically Christian sphere. In fact there were Jewish and Hellenistic sects even before the rise of the church: later Islam, too, experienced splinter groups.

A sectarian history runs parallel to the history of Christianity. Paul saw himself confronted with 'false teachers' and the faithful who clustered round them. Soon Gnostic communities spread whose adherents claimed a special illumination and election. Rigoristic reformers then split off from the mainstream church, claiming that it had become worldly and suffered moral decay: Montanists, Novatianists, Donatists, Priscillians and others, each of whom were named after their particular 'founder'. In the Middle Ages the brutal power politics of the papacy provoked the reaction of the 'pure': Albigensians, Cathars, Waldensians and later the protest of Wyclif and Hus. It was the same with Reformation Christianity: on the 'left wing' the various Anabaptists developed with a charismatic self-understanding. This splinter movement still exists today, as we can see in many places. Within this cultural sphere at the present day apocalyptic groupings are also coming into being which seek to save their souls through collective suicide. It is obvious that such excesses also provoke a defensive reaction from the state authorities.

2. Characteristics

We can see how varied the so-called 'sectarian scene' is, and at the same time how hard it is to define the nature of a sect clearly. It is at most possible to offer a phenomenological definition or description; some of its features must necessarily be blurred. For nothing would be more inaccurate than to use the same name both for peaceful communities of brothers and sisters outside the mainstream church and for people who manipulate others, or for avaricious and murderous groups.

An attempt at a phenomenology brings out the following characteristics:

- An emphatic concern to part company with the mainstream church, laying claim to being an alternative and exclusively true church.
- The appeal to the personality of a founder and teacher who is regarded as charismatic and is often acknowledged to have received illumination from special revelations.[45] To him is due unconditional obedience, and his writings have normative authority.
- A highly developed sense of election. Here belonging to the religious community is regarded as a condition of salvation: *'extra communitatem non est salus'* (no salvation outside the community').
- Little readiness for ecumenical dialogue, combined with a great readiness to propagate the group's own message of salvation and the biblical interpretation on which this is based.
- The mental manipulation of members, especially children. However, the latter is not claimed to be a general characteristic of sects; rather, it stems from a strong personal conviction of being in the truth.

Conclusion: perspectives on the future

As a Catholic theologian whose standpoint is that of Vatican II, I feel led to make the following prediction. Granted, it cannot be proved, but my assumption is that the communion of Christian churches – Catholic, Reformed and Orthodox – is capable of discovering authentic 'signs of the time' in the present religious 'chaos' which it has to interpret in the light of the gospel. In my view this chaos resembles the chaos the regularities of which are being investigated today in 'chaos theory' in physics, and is to be recognized as a phase of turbulence from which new possibilities of order can arise.[46]

If that is the case, then we can also reckon with the disappearance of the great anxiety within the church which today is leading to the introduction of authoritarian and centralistic regulations and condemnations in order to control what is supposed to be great religious 'disorder'. If the Spirit – which the Gospel of John says blows where it wills (John 3.8) – is in fact followed, then the conviction will prevail in our churches that the religious scene, which today is splintered and disordered, will automatically find a way to a new order and to a specifically modern unity in plurality. I personally hope very much for such an ecclesial 'self-organization' and 'evolution'.

That development will not be without risk and danger. Konrad Lorenz could already point out[47] that our 'globalized' civilization is demonstrating phenomena of an evolution backwards or a regression at lower levels. He also speaks, using a theological metaphor, of the 'deadly sins' of civilized humanity. Now world religion, including the Christian spontaneous communities and sects, is likewise exposed to the effect of such destructive forces.

Precisely for that reason we may hope for help from the teaching of the Council in the renewal which is necessary time and again. In the context of our topic this means that all the forms, both the great and institutional forms and the small, freely developing forms of the present-day church of God (*ekklesia tou theou*), will have time and again to measure themselves by the primitive Christian ideal or the gospel in order to arrive at a fruitful self-criticism.

This includes not least an intelligent, creative and bold strategy of inculturation, though this is not possible without a watchful openness to the world and a criticism of it. For we cannot baptize all that is religious and receive it into Christianity. Even the charisms, whether they manifest themselves within or outside the 'visible' community of the church, can be distorted and corrupted to the degree that they incarnate themselves in human capabilities. For that very reason Paul required that the authenticity and the appropriate use, for example, of the gift of prophecy had to be tested communally, indeed 'collegially', and judged. It is no good naively approving everything. On the other hand even semi-distorted charisms can bring about much good and express the will of God – thanks to the incorruptible spirit of God that is at work in them. This recognition therefore calls for tolerance and restraint in judging individual religious persons, particularly when these are members of sects. In the future it must be possible also to act ecumenically in this sphere. That means among other things that Christians should point out the importance of a degree of ecumenism even to their fellow men and women who are not that way inclined.

As well as many base communities which are inculturated in a different way, above all in Latin America, in my view the example of the French communities gives ground for hope. They aim in particular to build on the ecclesiology developed by the Council: to develop the local church which is understood in terms of its 'human location' and the particular church with its representative and qualitative ecclesiality in the communities of the charismatic renewal and with an eye to the Pauline 'house communities'. The 'community which meets in the house (*kat'oikon . . . ekklesia*) of' the lay people Prisca and Aquila (Rom. 16.5), in which the wife clearly exercises a ministry of leadership, will become especially topical in the future. The smallest ecclesial group as the core, nucleus, breeding ground, initial cell and basis[48] of the 'one, only, Catholic and apostolic church' (*una, sancta, catholica et apostolica*) seems to me to be that dynamic structure which promises us a qualitatively better future for the church. According to structural theory, men and women live after the model of 'structure in structures' or 'community in communities'. That is the only way in which organic growth comes about. In this way the church, too, constantly changes and is renewed. Some say 'from below'.

Over the next decades an atheism with a rational legitimation but which is also decadent and reductionist will continue to spread. On the other hand all kinds of religious and quasi-religious groups will mushroom. The mainstream churches and the world religions must not repudiate these but accept them as a challenge with a view to their own appropriate renewal. There is good reason to hope that in this way free competition with religionlessness and also among the religions and churches will also lead to an advancement of the human.

Translated by John Bowden

Notes

1. LG 13.3; 23.1; UR 2; AG 12. The following abbreviations are used: AA Decree on the Apostolate of Lay People, *Apostolicam actuositatem*; AG Decree on the Church's Missionary Activity, *Ad Gentes*; CD Decree on the Pastoral Office of Bishops in the Church, *Christus Dominus*; GS Pastoral Constitution on the Church in the Modern World, *Gaudium et Spes*; LG Dogmatic Constitution on the Church, *Lumen Gentium*; SC Constitution on the Sacred Liturgy, *Sacrosanctum Concilium*; UR Decree on Ecumenism, *Unitatis redintegratio*
2. 'vere *adest* /. . ./ *in omnibus legitimis fidelium congregationibus*'.
3. Acts 8.1; 14.22f. and 20.17.
4. See H. J. Klauck, *Hausgemeinde und Hauskirche im frühen Christentum*, Stuttgart 1981; R. Banks, *Paul's Idea of Community*, Exeter 1980.

5. E. Lanne, 'Die Ortskirche, ihre Katholizität und Apostolizität' in *Katholizität und Apostolizität, Kerygma und Dogma*, Beiheft 2, Göttingen 1971, pp. 129–51: 146.

6. Thus ibid., p. 147.

7. *Congregatio* or *communitas localis:* LG 26.1; 28.4; vgl. AG 19.2.

8. For the term see A. Ganoczy, 'Wesen und Wandelbarkeit der Ortskirche', *ThQ* 158, 1978, pp. 2–14: 10f.

9. Cf. UR 2, the title, and AG 19.1.

10. *Renovatio* – the Council uses the relevant word-group fifty times!

11. '*Novitas Jesu Christ*'; cf. LG 7.5; 40.2; 48.4; 56.

12. Cf. H. Mühlen, *Die Erneuerung des christlichen Glaubens, Charisma-Geist-Befreiung*, Munich 1974; id., *Geisterfahrung und Erneuerung*, Munich 1974.

13. Congar, *I Believe in the Holy Spirit I: The Experience of the Spirit*, London 1983, pp. 171ff.

14. Ibid.

15. Ibid.

16. Mühlen, *Erneuerung* (n. 12), p. 217. Congar speaks of 'gifts of nature and grace' (ibid.).

17. In what follows I am presenting the results of the research of Monique Hébrard, *Les nouveaux disciples. Dix ans après*, Paris 1987, here pp. 97, 107. See also A. Ganoczy, 'Communautés de vie in Frankreich als Ort theologischer Reflexion' in E. Klinger and R. Zerfass (eds), *Die Basisgemeinden – ein Schritt auf dem Weg zur Kirche des Konzils*, Würzburg 1984, pp. 32–42.

18. Hébrard, *Les nouveaux disciples* (n. 17), pp. 12, 37.

19. Ibid., p. 41.

20. Ibid., p. 54.

21. Ibid., p. 43.

22. Cf. ibid., p. 54, e.g. the community of 'The New Way'.

23. Cf. ibid., pp. 17, 48, 72.

24. Ibid., p. 72, e.g. the community of the 'Lion of Judah'.

25. Ibid., p. 17.

26. Ibid., pp. 25, 297.

27. Ibid., pp. 158.

28. Ibid., p. 304.

29. Ibid., pp. 16, 37, 75.

30. The relations between 'The New Way' and the archbishops of Lyons and Paris are important, cf. ibid., pp. 44, 54.

31. Ibid., p. 272.

32. Ibid., p. 274.

33. Cf. CELAM, Conclusiones de Medellin 1968, Doc. Pastoral de Conjunto no. 10.

34. Hébrard, *Les nouveaux disciples* (n. 17), p. 87.

35. Ibid., pp. 51–53.
36. Ibid., p. 286.
37. Ibid., p. 55.
38. Ibid., p. 72.
39. Ibid., pp. 132, 246.
40. Ibid., pp. 51f. on Bible study in 'The New Way'.
41. Ibid., p. 248.
42. Ibid., p. 180.
43. Cf. the articles 'Sekten, I. Religionsgeschichtlich (P. Honigsheim), II. Kirchen-geschichtlich (K. Schäferdiek)', *RGG* ³ V, 1658–61; 'Sekte', *LThK*² 9, 613–15 (K. Keinath).
44. Joint statement by the Catholic Bishops Conference and the Protestant Church Council on the French draft law on sects, *Le Monde*, 23 May 2001. The text criticizes the vagueness of the term sect which is used, but agrees with the protection of human rights intended by the law.
45. The accusation made by the Reformation churches of an 'expansion' of the biblical revelation belongs here.
46. See my *Chaos, Zufall, Schöpfungsglaube. Die Chaostheorie als Herausforderung der Theologie*, Mainz 1995, in which the last chapter (pp. 226–32) has the title 'Community between Chaos and Order'.
47. Cf. K. Lorenz, *Der Abbau des Menschlichen*, Munich and Zürich ²1983; id., *Die acht Todsünden der zivilisierten Menschheit*, Munich and Zurich ²²1990.
48. The Medellin document (no. 26) uses these metaphors.

Catholic Movements and Communities of the Faithful which arose in the Twentieth Century: Some Challenges to Canon Law

JEAN-PAUL DURAND

I. Protest or integration, protest and integration

Do certain foundations of movements and communities of Catholic faithful which arose in the twentieth century show signs of prophetism[1] or a Christian rigorism?[2] Be this as it may, Paul VI suffered from the reputation of mistrusting Catholic neo-Pentecostalism, while John Paul II is still sometimes criticized for having been too enthusiastic about initiatives towards associations which are 'supra-territorial' and cover 'many states of life' in the Roman Catholic Church. It will be for historians to assess the truth of these verdicts. It is for canon lawyers now to work out their significance for the institution, with all interested partners, whether religious or civil: there is a religious interest in these new spiritualities because the spiritual foundations can raise questions for all the Christian churches and all the religions in the world,[3] a world which culturally is still very diversified,[4] even if it is now said almost to have become one big village. There is also civil and political interest in these new spiritualities, because public order,[5] public health and public security are taking steps to discover if these new religious forms do not display tendencies towards sectarianism[6] or to proselytism of a doubtful kind,[7] or even to discover whether they represent new challenges of uncontrollable power,[8] or, better, whether they will be new stimuli towards humanization.[9] At the very heart of the most abysmal distress – world wars and regional wars, the Shoah, the Gulags, the Armenian genocide, world famine, AIDS, etc., a Christian mysticism has arisen again in the twentieth century the political scope of which has not escaped the best observers.[10]

Throughout the course of the history of the church of Christ, currents have arisen with both great energy for protest and a great power of integration, so that the world accepts the kingdom of God. Inevitably these currents always begin in a hesitant way[11]and without always being able to avoid mistakes: they are new shoots; they pierce a carpet of conformity to proclaim loudly that the church is not Christian enough, does not accord enough with the gospel, is not human enough. These currents do not become resigned when faced with a humankind which believes that it has been emancipated from God since the nineteenth cenury,[12] a humanity which knows how to teach religion philosophically as a problem.[13]

Be this as it may, groups are becoming impatient and shaking the edifice of the church, as if this great body of convictions[14] and rituals[15] did not know what to do faced with the challenges of the time: in mysticism,[16] in justice,[17] in ecology,[18] in biology[19] and anthropology,[20] in polemics,[21] in friendship,[22] in globalization,[23] in utopia.[24]

1. Mysticism or politics?

We know that the Catholic groups which came into being in the twentieth century do not form an absolutely homogenous phenomenon in origins and profiles. I shall not attempt to classify the theological and pastoral positions, for example into progressives and conservatives, or modernists and traditionalists. Not because these attributes are empty, but because certain forms of behaviour are more complex. Traditionalists can compromise with some parameters of modernity: for example Lefebvre's integralist association St Pius X has not hesitated to defend its conception of truth and authority by making use of the 1905 civil statute on religious associations, though this was forbidden to Catholics by Pius X. And when it comes to classifying Catholic movements and communities which have arisen in the twentieth century on the chessboard of politics it is necessary to take account of countries and periods; sometimes great causes separate the members of the same community in a profound way. In the course of the twentieth century and above all in France, Catholicism and its more militant groupings did not succeed in forming a homogeneous political current, but the episcopates, Catholic movements and indeed the pope were convinced that there was a place for the spiritual and moral authorities in the political, economic, social and cultural debate.[25]

Granted, the American historian Dale K. Van Kley has recently put forward the thesis that revolutions will always be religious.[26] Formerly Jansenism could appear as a substitute for Protestantism by virtue of its pessimistic theology of grace; however, Jansenism is distinguished by its attachment to the church as a mediating authority and as a community which transcends the individual conscience.[27] For France, van Kley proposes a new view of the religious roots of the 1789 Revolution: his proposal does not just consist of recalling that the lower clergy supported the first steps of this revolution but in showing that the anti-monarchical and even anti-religious elements in the Revolution were due not so much to the rationalism of the Enlightenment as to the Protestant and Jansenist dissent which was so fought against by the monarchy in the seventeenth and eighteenth centuries.

In France at least, 'the separation' – in the sense of a distinction between the spheres of political and the confessions – ended up haunting the Catholic conscience, but that was not without its painful aspect: one might think of the refusals formulated by the majority of French Catholics to the invitation made by Pope Leo XIII in 1892 in the hope that they would rally to the Republic by civism, a political regime which became the legitimate regime of France. However, figures like Bienheureux Frédéric Ozanam (1813–53) had already been able to find a better theological motive for social involvement, out of the rut of counter-revolutionary resentment.[28] In reality, the Catholic intellectuals who were born around 1880–90 in France, Belgium and Switzerland primarily wanted to be both Thomists and Maurrasians, in a twofold context: that of the French victory in 1918 and the spiritual crisis which characterized the period following the First World War. 1926 was the year of the papal condemnation of *Action française*: at that time many Catholics had to choose between loyalty to Rome and loyalty to Maurras, two loyalties which hitherto had been perceived as complementary and which had been made incompatible by the condemnation. Mention must also be made of the roots existing between le Sillon and the founders of Catholic workers' action (*Jeunesse ouvrière chrétienne*: JOC).

Notably in France, movements and communities of Catholic faithful and the congregational communities of the twentieth century were looking for a new intervention in the relationship between human history and the history of salvation: this quest also runs across the diocesan churches and their clergy, the secular character and apostolic nature of which also aimed at becoming bound up in a renewed symbiosis.[29]

2. Contrasting appeals for a new reform of Catholicism?

A contemplative Thomist philosophical leader like Jacques Maritain beyond question inspired a vast investigation, extending far beyond Francophone cultures, which led to the invention of ways of temporal Christian hope that respected the primacy of the spiritual, ways that could lead the way to contemplation of the transcendence of the message of the gospel in relationship to Western civilization, and of the need to subordinate political action to the demands of morality.[30] Thus a number of Catholics sought a renewal of involvement in the life of the city, in the name of the imperatives of Christian morality. These moves were to have repercussions on French society in particular[31] and on the contribution of its culture to the preparation of Vatican II and the evolution of Catholicism.

In my view, the springing up of small, especially neo-Pentecostalist, communities in France[32] after Vatican II has not changed the fundamental facts in this relationship – renewed between 1914 and the end of the Algerian war – , a relationship which French Catholicism maintains, albeit in an increasingly disintegrating way, with civil society; it is a relationship from now on thought of and lived out in terms of separation between the state jurisdictions and the confessional jurisdictions.[33]

The twentieth century has seen the establishment all over the world of the usual forms of communities practising the religious life and movements of spirituality and apostolate for the laity. It has always been necessary to find a balance between the primacy accorded by tradition to the principle of territoriality for the corporate bodies of a hierarchical nature with apostolic power, a primacy over non-territorial ecclesial forms: this principle of territoriality was brought out at the Colloquium of the World Association of Canonists in Budapest in September 2001.[34]

II. Territorial and non-territorial forms

But the twentieth century has also seen the birth of quite new forms of the evangelical life and the quest for a Christian life: the different canonical states of life are sometimes invited to live together in the same community – communal life. It may happen that there are other situations in which the baptized and the non-baptized, men and women, may be associated. I shall not describe all these situations, nor can I present here an exhaustive typology of the movements and communities which arose in the twentieth century. But I note the existence of a principle which is often realized, or at least sought, namely the principle of communities composed of people belonging to different canonical states of life, indeed ecclesial situations which are not canonical or are difficult.

Thus various people can seek to co-operate together: catechumens, celibate men and women of different ages who are not religious (problems arise over the status and freedom of minors); so too can those who have taken religious vows; rarely, certain homosexuals and lesbians in relationships can co-operate; sometimes there are unmarried couples, and often couples who have been married in a civil and/or religious ceremony, spouses separated canonically, abandoned spouses, divorcees who have not remarried or who have; widows and widowers are present; ordained secular ministers also co-operate in different ways; finally there can be co-operation between some who have been excommunicated, since excommunication is a canonical penal status according to which a baptized person is deprived of the sacraments for a certain time to lead him or her to penance. It is an existential and spiritual matter, when the church makes the firm demand that these penitents should change personally as soon as possible, preferably inwardly, before God and the church. Baptized non-Catholics, indeed believers of other religions and even non-believers engaged in a spiritual, philosophical, ethical and aesthetic quest, can join groups of Catholic faithful which sometimes have a communal life.

The non-territorial forms of the gospel quest – whether or not recognized canonically, or recognized to different degrees – have always been part of the history of the church and of its great territorial institutions, namely the churches *sui iuris*,[35] the ecclesiastical provinces, the metropolitan arch-dioceses, the dioceses,[36] some territorial prelatures and abbeys, the parishes and the chaplaincies. The history of Christianity is also criss-crossed by a quest for a balance between the ministerial priesthood and the communal priesthood of the faithful. Above all following the gospel movements of the twelfth century and even more the crisis of the Protestant Reformation from the sixteenth century onwards, the history of the church has been even more marked by a quest for a balance between the different canonical states of life and even between non-canonical forms of life of the baptized.

I prefer not to use the expression 'new communities', since it is too precise, too provisional. Canonists are working on their status in canon law.[37] Some of these movements and groups of the faithful who live a common life have no difficulty in seeking a canonical status of an associative nature in civil and in canon law. There is a regime codified by the church of associations of private canon law.[38]

1. Associations of canon law?

Sometimes the question of their access to the regime of association in public canon law is raised, by the apostolic authority of the diocese, by the conference of bishops or by the Holy See, or by the movements and communities themselves. We know that this regime gives the apostolic authority more powers over the government and the possessions of these associations of faithful. The canonical tradition requires them to be established as legal persons in public canon law, which have an object *in nomine Ecclesiae*: these are primarily tangible objects, namely presenting the word of God, the liturgy, catechesis, but also engaging in charitable works, Catholic education and other works of general cultural interest and humanitarian works, after receiving the proper Catholic confessional character from the competent canonical authority.

Some of these associations of faithful want to devote themselves to the training of future ordained ministers. This raises tricky problems. The classical institution of the seminaries, which emerged from the Council of Trent, bears witness to the difficulty of the task which certain communities of the faithful want also to assume from now on. Associations of faithful ask to be able to support ordained ministers in their ministry. The Neocatechumenal Way has long sought a canonical status with Rome, knowing that sometimes dioceses and parishes have been able to allow some their first steps: how is it possible to avoid ways which are too parallel at the heart of parishes or in the life of a whole diocese?

2. Lay movements

Movements of the faithful which include some communal life for some of their members do not want above all to be assimilated to a form of religious life, nor to be laity governed by a deacon, a priest or a prelate bishop. By vocation these movements want to be lay and to make themselves available so that they are capable of offering their service, individually or communally, both for humanitarian works or for the apostolate: for example Fondacio (for a new world) can arrange co-operation between the lay apostolate both inside and outside France with particular dioceses or conferences of bishops and with the Pontifical Council for the laity.

Movements and communities of faithful have within them different canonical states of life, but in a more or less distinct and institutionalized way, as in the charismatic Community of the New Way.[39] Only some of its members – laity, both married and unmarried, with a few religious – share a common life, while a male religious institute has been established by a metropolitan archbishop. In civil law, the part of the Community of the New Way which leads a common life – cohabitation in the broad sense – has asked for and obtained from the French civil authorities legal recognition as a religious congregation, while the male religious institute has not asked this of the state.[40]

3. 'New forms of religious life'

Some communities of the faithful receive canonical recognition as 'new forms of the religious life' provided for by canon 605 of the Latin Code of 1983.[41] We know that for the first time a universal canon law provides for future forms of religious life; John Paul II has wanted to draw the attention of diocesan bishops to possible foundations in search of a religious life, whether Latin or Eastern (canon 571, CCEO 1990). It seems so far that only two institutes have been approved by pontifical law so far, under this canon 605. What aspects mark these institutes out as new? For example, a study of the Society of Christ the Lord in Montreal shows that religious men and women are members of the same religious institute with one and the same superior ('supreme moderator'). If associations of faithful are made up of lay people and priests, the canonical tradition wants the canonical superior to be a priest. The canonical tradition also requires an association whose members, male and female, pronounce all the private vows of celibacy for the kingdom of God, not to have the right to see their community, which leads a common life, established as a single religious institute of the religious life if it is governed jointly by the men and women of the same community.

That is the case with the missionary association for the faithful, *Redemptor hominis*, founded by a mission priest from Rome: it was established as a canonical association of faithful by a Dutch diocesan bishop. Then it set up the centre for the initial training of its members – men and women consecrated by private vows – in a diocese in Cameroon. All these situations express a quest for a life shared by men and women, including those who are committed by private vows of celibacy to the kingdom of God. This quest for chastity in celibacy within mixed groups leading a common life is an aspect which is now welcomed more warmly. Sometimes in the Middle Ages there was such a jurisdiction, exercised by an abbess over a monastery of men. Likewise, there are still sometimes institutionalized neighbourly relationships between a male monastery and a female convent, belonging to a spiritual family, like a monastic order.

Movements of the faithful have also sought to reconcile social work, including work at the international level, with a community of religious life and lay Christian life: in Italy there is Comunione and Liberation[42] and the

Sant' Egidio community.[43] These communities know that their vocation is not to be a substitute for the traditional life of the dioceses, nor do they have the function of nunciatures: the large communities or movements are specific supports so that the church can perform its mission with the necessary flexibility,[44] as it faces the great challenges of the age.

Other foundations have had to explore their canonical identity through history to discover whether they were both monasteries and particular churches, like the abbeys *nullius*. The church has found the formula for prelatures and retained the territorial prelature among the particular churches. As for Opus Dei, which claims the status of a particular church, the 1983 Latin Code of Canon Law has assigned it the special regime of a personal prelature, without putting it formally on the list of different particular churches.

III. The challenges of modernity

Faced with the challenges of modernity and its crises, faced with sometimes very esoteric religious demands, and certainly faced with harsh attacks in Catholicism, in their own way, in their impatience and – I would stress once again – in a very contrasting manner – the foundations of faithful in the twentieth century, the context of which has been described in this article, indicate reforms to be made and principles to be reaffirmed. Some trends in Catholicism expect a great deal of a new ecumenical council; others put themselves forward bluntly as alternative forms of ecclesial life, above traditional territorial structures which are thought to be too complicated and heavy. But the canonists know that the radicalized option of personal churches has always been judged to be too communitarian or too ideological. Certainly the territorial option has asked the churches to engage in difficult dealings, in particular with the nations.[45]

At all events, difficulties, inadequacies and failures too are not lacking within the foundations of faithful in the twentieth century.[46] Many of the apostolic and contemplative religious institutes, the traditional forms of communal life, have had crises of recruitment and restructuring. The secular institutes, too, have attempted several breakthroughs.[47] From the side of the territorial institutions, have the openings brought about by Vatican II, and the forms of participation offered by the Latin Codex of Canon Law and the Codex of the Eastern Churches been sufficiently welcomed? Such lacks can put a brake on dialogue and co-operation between young foundations and old institutions. Occasions for dialogue remain a dead letter, like the particular canonical right of a diocesan and the conference of bishops to take an initiative: these occasions which might provide a dynamic have so far remained in very puny forms, while the canonical work of adaptation and enculturation is immense. Likewise the virtual absence of provincial councils can be noted: this threatens to isolate episcopal animation from the rest of the regional church, from certain young foundations and from civil society. Other intermediaries exist, but are we not seeing certain diocesan synodal processes running out of steam, sometimes without sufficient capacity to make a decision? Despite some efforts, one has to deplore the rarity of diocesan catechisms. And this at a time when a word of pastoral and doctrinal help should be supporting prayer, worship and truth and acts of charity and brotherhood in the face of contemporary ethical challenges. Moreover, does not the preparation of some young priests – who are already rare, but sometimes very clerical – contrast with the sharing of pastoral responsibilities which awaits many of them? Moreover, the continued timidity in dialogue with Westernized women over freedom and responsibility in the media, culture and family work is to be deplored.[48] Unless sufficient debates are begun in the church, types of 'parallel churches' will multiply.

Translated by John Bowden

Notes

1. Jean Séguy, *Conflit et utopie ou réformer l'Eglise, parcours wébérien en douze essais*, Collection Sciences humaines et religions, Paris 1999.

2. Jean-Louis Quantin, *Le rigorisme chrétien*, Collection Histoire du christianisme, Paris 2001, p. 163.

3. René Simon (ed), 'Ethique et mystique (I, II)', *Revue d'éthique et de théologie morale 'Le Supplément'* (= *RETM*) 212, March-April 2000, pp. 5–44, and p. 214, September 2000, pp. 9–120; Bruno Duffé (ed), 'Le dialogue interreligieux: une provocation à la réflexion éthique et théologique?', *RETM* 217, June-July 2001, pp. 7–214.

4. Michel Istas, *Les morales selon Max Weber*, Collection Histoire de la morale, Paris 1986.

5. *L'ordre public*, Collection Travaux de l'association Henri Capitant, Journées libanaises tome XLIX, Paris 1998.

6. Like many sociologists and jurists I try to take care to avoid slipping into the ideological usage of the word 'sect'. Its moralism does not aid the discernment presupposed by an enlightened struggle against attacks that could be committed by groups against human beings and their dignity. Cf. Francis Messner

(ed), *Les 'sectes' et le droit en France*, Collection Politique d'aujourd'hui, Paris 1999; *Les nouveaux mouvements religieux et le droit dans l'Union européenne* (Consortium européen pour l'étude des relations Eglises-Etat), Milan 1999; Jean-Paul Durand, 'La loi du 12 juin 2001 de prévention et de répression des "mouvements sectaires"', *L'année canonique* 41, 2001, pp. 309–22; Françoise Champion, 'Sectes et démocratie', Colloque international Droits de l'homme et liberté de religion: pratiques en Europe occidentale (II), *Conscience et liberté* 62, 2001, pp.163–68. Instead of speaking of 'sects' to denote minorities, the less well known confessional denominations have to be able to rely on a non-discriminatory public order: Jean Seguy, 'Menno Simons, réformateur du XVIᵉ siècle' in *Menno Simons, Actes du colloque du 12 octobre 1996 à Hautefeuille*, Saint Maurice (94410), Mission mennonite française, 1997, pp. 3–28.

7. A thesis on the notion of proselytism to be defended by Philippe Greiner in Paris.

8. François Champion and Martine Cohen (eds), *Sectes et démocratie*, Paris 1999.

9. Xavier Thévenot, *Compter sur Dieu, études de théologie morale*, Collection Recherches morales-positions, Paris 1993.

10. Bertrand Saint-Sernin, *L'action politique selon Simone Weil*, Collection Histoire de la morale, Paris 1988.

11. Jean-Paul Durand (ed), 'Communautés nouvelles et nouveaux mouvements religieux dans l'Eglise catholique d'aujourd'hui', *L'année canonique* 36, 1993, pp. 13–130 ; 'Une communauté charismatique dialogue avec des théologiens moralistes', *RETM* 65, June 1988, pp. 5–47.

12. Pierre Viaud, *Une humanité affranchie de Dieu au XIX siècle, recherche d'un ordre universel*, Collection Histoire de la morale, Paris 1994.

13. Jean Greisch, *Le buisson ardent et les lumières de la raison, l'invention de la philosophie de la religion, Tome 1, Héritages et héritiers du XIX siècle*, Collection Philosophie et théologie, Paris 2002.

14. Peter Huizing et William Basset (eds), 'Croire sur commande? Problèmes juridiques autour du Magistère', *Concilium* 117, 1976 (not published in English); Bernard Sesboüé, *Le magistère à l'épreuve*, Paris 2001; Xavier Lacroix et Jean-Paul Durand (eds), 'La notion de Magistère ordinaire et universel', *RETM* 319, December 2001, pp. 11–66 ; Jean-Paul Durand (ed), 'Adhérer aux enseignements d'Eglise', *RETM* 216, March-April 2001, pp. 5–54.

15. Bernard Kaempf (ed), *Rites et ritualités*, Collection Théologies pratiques, Paris 2000.

16. Guy Michelat, 'L'essor des croyances parallèles' in *Futuribles*, no. 260, January 2001, pp. 61–72; Roland Maisonneuve, *Les mystiques chrétiens et leurs visions de Dieu un et trine*, Collection Patrimoines christianisme, Paris 2000.

17. See the post-Communist discussions on the one hand and those about the development of the thought of John Rawls, for example his 1999 work *The Law of People*. I cannot emphasize too much the message of Madeleine Delbrêl:

Jean-Paul Durand et Jean Gueguen (eds), 'Les communistes et les chrétiens, alliance ou dialogue ? Madeleine Delbrêl (1904–1933–1964)', *RETM* 173, June 1990; Jean Gueguen (ed), 'Madeleine Delbrêl, la justice à l'épreuve', *RETM* 198, 1996.

18. Francis Rollin (ed), 'Environnement, création, éthique', *RETM* 169, June 1989.

19. 'La vie humaine sur le marché' in *Les petites affiches* 243, 5 December 2002.

20. Geneviève Delaisi de Parseval, *Le roman familial d'Isadora D.*, Paris 2002.

21. Pierre M. Gallois, *Le devoir de vérité*, Paris 2002.

22. Jean-Marie Gueullette (ed), 'Accompagner l'autre. Quelles évolutions ? Quels repères éthiques?', *RETM* 222, September 2002, pp. 21–298.

23. 'Mondialistes autrement', *Spiritus* 166, March 2002.

24. Gilles Curien, *Aujourd'hui la fin des temps*, Collection Parole présente, Paris 2000.

25. Brigitte Vassort-Rousset, *Les évêques de France en politique*, Collection Sciences humaines des religions, Paris 1986; Dominique Greiner, 'La parole des Eglises dans le champ de l'économie', *RETM* 210, September 1999, pp. 151–72; Paul J. Fitzgerald, 'Quand la doctrine sociale catholique rencontre la religion civile nord-américaine sur l'économique' (1986), *RETM* 220, March 2002, pp. 79–100; Edouard Bonnefous and Patrick Valdrini (eds), *La société dans les encycliques de Jean Paul II*, Paris 2000; Philippe Levillain, 'La Papauté entre guerres et paix' in Edouard Bonnefous, Joel Benoot d'Onorio et Jean Foyer (eds), *La Papauté au XX siècle*, Paris 1999.

26. Jacqueline Lalouette, *La République anticléricale XIX-XX siècle*, Collection L'univers historique, Paris 2002.

27. Commentary by André Burguière on the work of Dale K. Van Kley, *Les origines religieuses de la Révolution française, 1560–1791*, Paris 2002.

28. Bernard Barbiche (ed), 'Frédéric Ozanam, intellectuel catholique', *Revue d'histoire de l'Eglise de France* 85, January-June 1999.

29. Nathalie Viet-Depaule (ed), *La mission de Paris, cinq prêtres-ouvriers insoumis témoignent*, Paris 2002.

30. Philippe Chenaux, *Entre Maurras et Maritain, une génération intellectuelle catholique (1920–1930)*, Collection Sciences humaines et religions, Paris 1999.

31. Jean-Yves Calvez, *Chrétiens penseurs du social, Maritain, Mounier, Fessard, Teilhard de Chardin, de Lubac*, Collection Histoire de la morale, Paris 2002.

32. Jean-René Bouchet and Henri Caffarel, *Le Renouveau charismatique interpellé, études et documents*, Collection Renouveau 5, Paris 1976; Juan-Miguel Garrigues, Marcel Bourland, Laurent Fabre et al., *Présence du Renouveau charismatique*, Collection Chemin neuf, Paris 1979.

33. René Rémond, *Une mémoire française, entretiens avec Marc Leboucher*, Paris 2002.

34. Forthcoming.

35. Elias Sleman, 'De "Ritus" à "ecclesia sui iuris" dans le Code des canons des Eglises orientales', *L'année canonique* XLI, 1999, pp. 253–78.

36. Gérald Chaix (ed), *Le diocèse, espaces, représentations, pouvoirs, France, XV-XX siècle*, Collection Histoire religieuse de la France, Paris 2002; Richard Kulimushi Mutarushwa, *La charge pastorale, droit universel et droit local*, Collection Droit canonique, Paris 1999.

37. Giorgio Feliciani, 'Quel statut canonique pour les nouvelles communautés?', *L'année canonique* XLII, 2000, pp. 151–66.

38. Lius Nararro, 'Les sujets nés de l'initiative des fidèles et de la personnalité juridique privée', *L'année canonique*, XLI, 1999, pp. 201–28.

39. See the memorandum and the thesis by Juan Echeverria, Institut catholique, Paris and Gregorian, Rome 1999.

40. Jean-Paul Durand, *La liberté religieuse des congrégations religieuses en France*, Collection Droit canonique et droit civil ecclésiastique, Paris 1999 (3 vols).

41. Marie Aleth Trapet, *Le ministère de discernement de l'évêque face aux recherches nouvelles de vie consacrée, interprétation et réception du canon 605 du Code de droit canonique*, typescript thesis, Paris 1986.

42. Salvatore Abbruzzese, *Comunie e liberazine, identité catholique et disqualification du monde*, Collection Sciences humaines et religions, Paris 1998.

43. Its influence necessarily made one of the great journals there, not least to emphasize its influence; Andrea Riccardi, 'Rome est un lieu idéal pour se rencontrer, Dossier: Comment le Vatican pèse sur les affaires du monde', *Le Monde*, Thursday 26 December 2002, p. 2.

44. Vincent Hanicotte, *Le caract?re religieux d'une activité par nature professionnelle, exercée dans le cadre d'un engagement cultuel: lien communautaire et droit du travail dans les collectivités religieuses*, Mémoire de DEA, typescript thesis, Institut catholique, Paris and University of Paris XI, 1999.

45. Jean-Paul Durand, 'Colloque sur les Eglises nationales', *L'année canonique*, 43, 2001, pp. 4–118.

46. I would like to recall all the community failures of Christian life: Olivier Braconnier, *Radiographie d'une secte au-dessus de tout soupçon ou l'histoire mouvementée du groupe de Saint-Erme*, Collection Rencontres, Paris 1982.

47. Marie-Antoinette Perret, *Une vocation paradoxale, les instituts séculiers féminins en France (XIX-XX siècles)*, Collection Histoire, Paris 2000.

48. Jean-Marie Aubert, *L'exil féminin, antiféminisme et christianisme*, Collection Recherches morales, Paris 1988.

IV. Challenges

'Catholicism by way of Sectarianism?' An Old Hypothesis for New Problems

LUCA DIOTALLEVI

It is clear what has to be the first question: is there a widespread diffusion of sectarianism within Catholicism?[1] And are perhaps the 'movements' recognized[2] by the church the phenomena in which this tendency is making itself particularly evident?

I. 'Catholicism by way of sectarianism?' The question and its sociological implications

Especially, but not only, in the case of the 'movements' an unprecedented tendency is spreading which has not been prevalent in the tradition before. The primacy of territoriality as a criterion of segmentation within the church (diocese, parishes), a primacy connected with the fundamentally inclusive character of Catholicism, based on a 'non-élitist' belonging as a typical manifestation of the religion of the church, is taking new form.

1. Religious pluralism

If we reverse the perspective, in other words if we adopt the point of view of the faithful and not that of the institutions, we are forced to ask ourselves in what contexts it is still possible for the faithful to have a religious experience 'of the church' which can be observed socially. In what conditions can they still have an experience of the *una sancta* in a way that is socially relevant? Or are they destined to participate only in a 'little church', sometimes understood as the one pure church, and at others simply chosen as the dispenser of the most convenient religious product? Can we still also distinguish empirically, as in the past, a religious belonging of an ecclesial kind from all the other types of religious belonging of a non-religious kind? Or do religious belonging and participation also stand within belonging to the Catholic Church and religious participation of a non-ecclesial kind, consequently transforming the church into a simple and inevitably superficial accumulation of these fragmentary belongings?

2. Sociological implications

When we ask whether there are different orientations and sectarian styles in a church we are adopting the classical scheme in the sociology of religion of 'church and sect'. According to this scheme, 'church' and 'sect' are concepts which refer to two opposed models of religious organizations. Church and sect are both religious organizations, but they are religious organizations the main dimensions of which are opposed in a regime of almost perfect mutual exclusivity: as opposed in one genre. For some time, in fact, the sociology of religion has noted that religious organizations are either 'churches' or 'sects'. Then other types are added: 'denominations', 'cults', 'movements' etc. However, none of the definitions of these last has ever reached the precision of the first two, nor has their introduction in itself cancelled the relationship of opposition between them.

So from a sociological perspective it seems to me legitimate and useful to spell out at least three assumptions implied in the initial question.

(a) The church is a religious organization.
(b) The church is a religious organization the principal characteristics of which are opposed to that of the type of religious organization known as the 'sect': we have an inclusive as opposed to an exclusive character, territorial membership as opposed to élite membership, different processes of control and maintaining internal consensus, techniques of diffusion, etc.[3]

In the third place there is no denying the profound connection which exists between the classical 'church–sect' scheme and the classical version of the theory of secularization,[4] which today is often called the old paradigm. It is in fact somewhat difficult to adopt the 'church–sect' scheme without also assuming, more or less explicitly, a certain type of approach to the problematical relationship between modernization and religion. In fact the adoption of this scheme comprises the idea that

(c) the process of modernization tends to marginalize the social manifestations of religion or at least those of the 'church-orientated religions'.
In the contexts of advanced modernization, this thrust towards marginalization is opposed with a limited degree of efficacy only by the sects.

In short, to investigate a possible sectarian evolution of Catholicism is
also to assume – as a *terminus a quo* – a concept of the church (a) as a specific
religious organization, (b) as a religious organization characterized by the
prevalence of structural features which are inclusive and bureaucratic, (c) as
a religious organization which has few chances of success in the face of the
challenge of the modernization of society.

II. The growing analytical uselessness of the 'church-sect' scheme

From a sociological perspective the question of the possibility of an increas-
ing sectarianization of Catholicism, even through its 'movements', presents
some difficulties. In fact the sociology of religion has stopped talking about
churches, sects and more generally of religious organizations, and is resorting less and less to the opposition between church and sect to describe
different models of religious organization which are opposed in tendency.

1. A departure from the idea of secularization

J. Beckford[5] among others had already come to the conclusion that a mora-
torium should be called on the use of this classical scheme, now inadequate
for covering the variety of the population of the religious organizations.
F.-X. Kaufmann had also shared this view.[6] Similar comments then also
came from, among others, R. Wuthnow,[7] B.Wilson,[8] and D. Hervieu-
Léger.[9]

   If empirical analysis has found itself progressively forced to give up the
pretentious church-sect scheme, theoretical elaboration has also moved in
parallel in the same direction. For various reasons, which I hope will soon
become evident, it seems to me to be useful to draw attention to at least some
of the analytical instruments developed by Niklas Luhmann.[10] Among other
things, his contribution has the advantage of venturing an analysis of religion which is not separate from other social analysis.[11] Luhmann is positive
about not reducing the church to an organization (cf. [a]); no longer setting
church and sect over against each other as opposite genres – the genre of reli-

gious organizations (cf. [b]); and taking critically the departure from the old paradigm and its old idea of secularization without supporting illusions about a 'return of the sacred' and a 'desecularization' ([c]).

The main characteristic of advanced modernization,[12] understood as a global society,[13] is the multidimensional process of social differentiation dominated by the principle of the differentiation of society by functions.[14] The most relevant phenomenon is thus that individual specialized sub-systems form in society to guarantee a specific social function: politics, the family, the economy, science, religion, etc.[15] This transformation tremend-ously increases the complexity and contingency which are socially tolerable and, in accordance with an aspect on which attention must be firmly focussed, calls for a quite unprecedented differentiation between the differ-ent types of social systems (or 'social levels'): interactions, organizations, societies. Moreover, according to an intuition of Simmel's,[16] in this context this very process produces an enormous increment of differentiation between psychological and social systems, between persons and social sys-tems, and between religious feeling and religion.[17] In particular, here the light thrown by Luhmann on the differentiation between organization and societies, between communications in general and those communications which support decisions, proves useful.[18]

2. Religion as a sub-system of society

In a society the modernization of which is advanced, in the globalized society, not only is politics less dependent on the economy, the economy on politics, religion on politics, politics on religion, and so on, but no economic organization can determine the value of currency, no individual political organization can determine the law, and in general no individual organiza-tion which also works within a functionally specialized sub-system can maintain full control over the law which regulates this sub-system.[19]

It is particularly important that one aspect of the form assumed by the sub-systems of society arises in a society differentiated by functions, each of which is – increasingly – globalized. Politics, economics, science, religion, etc. have become such complex social realities that each of them proves completely incapable of being organized as a whole. At the same time they have become social functions for the performance of which the number, the variety and the quality of the necessary organizations has reached un-imagined and elevated thresholds even in the recent past.[20] Also only with reference to the beginnings of modernity, society in an advanced state of modernization and each of its functions have become social systems which are completely incapable of organization, and phenomenon which experience an unprecedented need for organizations. As I have said, that is also true of religion.[21] The number and type of religious organizations are growing (*pace* all the theories on the privatization of religions and the decline in the organizations and social institutions of religion), and – not 'but'! – the function of religion has its own social profile which is completely incapable of organization and is therefore incapable of being reduced, even just at the local level, to an organization or a complex of organizations.

As I have already remarked, that does not mean that the religious organizations do not influence the religious phenomena of a social type and vice versa.[22] It simply means that there is a growth in the *relative* autonomy between organizations and society and their *relative* heterogeneity. No economic organization can control the value attributed to the currency in monetary exchange (in economic communications); no political organization can any longer determine absolutely the 'content' of the positive law, and in fact we are now beyond the state. No religious organization can maintain complete control of the codes which regulate religious communication. Obviously this does not mean that all the organizations have the same influence on society. The decisions of the Federal Reserve have more influence on the movement of currency than the decisions of the Banca d'Italia; one scientific journal has more influence on the standard of scientific communication than another; and the Vatican bureaucracy has more influence on the dynamic and forms of religious communication than other religious organizations.

To sum up: the regime of differentiation between social functions which characterizes a society in an advanced state of modernization and the consequent increase in the differentiation both between organizations and societies and between social power and personal power already make the 'church–sect' scheme inadequate. It also rules out the idea that there can be organizations (in this case religious organizations) which are in a position to cancel the effect of such a state of affairs on themselves and their members, either by claiming (as do the classical organizations 'of the church') to control the whole religious system, even if only in a small area, or by claiming (as do the classical organizations of 'the sect') to guard against the impact of this social order on the life and the choices of its members.

Advanced modernization in society is advanced differentiation. Advanced differentiation before the decline of religion is an increment in the specialization of religion and in the religious system and between religion and religious sensibility. That obviously does not mean that there cannot be very influential organizations throughout the religious system and the rest of society, but sometimes a choice has to be made; nor does it mean that it is impossible to lead a life 'with a religious orientation', but only that – socially speaking – this cannot happen completely in the form of a simple application on the part of the individual of predetermined cognitive schemes and normative prescriptions.[23] Social relevance is something that the religious systems have constantly to regain,[24] personal religious life as a socially relevant phenomenon can now be led only through freedom and choice. That is the only course, for everyone, in a manifest way of which they are painfully aware. This is where the novelty lies.[25]

3. The church in a differentiated society

From a sociological perspective, what is the church in a functionally differentiated society? No social phenomenon, not even a religious phenomenon, can now also only be reduced even remotely to its organizational dimension. That puts in question the classical 'church-sect' scheme. So in a functionally differentiated society, are there observable and relevant religious phenomena which still prove useful in defining the 'church'?

We could begin to answer the question about what the/a church is in a society in an advanced state of modernization, or the conditions in which it is possible and useful to define a type of religious tradition as an ecclesial form, on the basis of phenomenological considerations. In connection with the breadth and internal complexity of the religious sub-system of a society differentiated by functions there are religious traditions which tend to develop in all directions and others which by contrast maximize their forces only in some directions, or even put themselves in particular niches. For example, it is evident that in the West there are religious traditions which are barely articulated and have little influence at the level of society (one might think of the denominations), and it is equally evident how here and above all in the East there are individualizable religious traditions which are less systematic than others but also structure themselves in an organized form. In the case of Catholicism, however, I think that it is evident how after some initial resistance, the challenge of advanced social modernization has been met today on both the social and also the organizational level.[26] More generally, the Catholic religious tradition tends to give itself the same breadth and the same complexity of religious system.

If, however, moving from the phenomenological to the theoretical level, we looked in Luhmann for a response to the question about the church as a sociological concept, we would find something that could perhaps be even more surprising. 'Church' is the concept to which the manifestations of religion are reduced at the level of society.[27] 'Church' here denotes any form of specifically religious communication.

What I have said should be enough to indicate that both from a phenomenological and a theoretical point of view there are good reasons for asserting that in a society with a high degree of modernization a 'church' *has* organizations but never *is* an organization. That should also be enough to help us to understand better some of the motives which now so tell against the use of the 'church-sect' scheme (cf. [b]) and the understanding of the church as a religious organization of a certain type (cf. [a]). What we can rightly call church today and what perhaps we could still call sect are no longer in a relationship of mutual exclusivity; they are not opposed in the same genre.

In terms of the history of sociological thought, too,[28] this shift of meaning in the concept of the 'church' can have good reasons. For example, it is not contradicted by the fact that in a social phase marked by less functional differentiation and thus of less differentiation between social and organizational systems, the church in Europe appears as a macro-organization.

Obviously, precisely because we can have religious traditions with an ecclesial form and others without such a form, to abandon the old concept of the church as an organization does not mean abandoning the possibility of still distinguishing between ecclesiastical religious organizations – bound up with religious traditions and institutions of an ecclesial kind – and non-ecclesiastical religious organizations. Consequently within a population of ecclesiastical organizations, for example Catholic organizations, we can find more exclusive (some 'movements') and less exclusive ones; we can also find some which make higher demands on entering and leaving than others. Nevertheless, I do not think that it is helpful, nor is it theoretically or even philologically an advantage, to call the former sects and the latter churches (cf. [b]).

4. Surviving in a globalized society

As empirical research is showing increasingly clearly,[29] and as Luhmann among others has tried to explain on the theoretical level, there is nothing in principle to indicate that religion will not continue to be able to cope with a globalized society in an advanced state of modernization. Religion can survive in the form of a specialized social system to whose code organizations and interactions refer. For the religious system, no more and no less than for the economic system, the political system or others, the necessity in the internal and external environment to confront the highest level of social complexity/contingency calls for a mix of inclusiveness (societal) and exclusiveness (organizational), and there is need for a capacity for synchronic and diachronic alternation between the inflationary management of the religious communicative code (typical of the more 'liberal' Christian tendencies) and its deflationary management (typical of the more 'fundamentalist' and 'sectarian' Christian tendencies).

In the religious system, as once again also in the political and economic system or in others, there are religious interests and traditions which point to a niche and – with all the infinite intermediary gradations – religious interests and traditions which give an orientation to all the dynamics of the sub-system. Above all in this second case, which is certainly also that of Catholicism, to be surprised at the presence of 'liberal' and/or 'fundamentalist' or 'sectarian' religious politics would be equivalent to being surprised because an economic or political interest did not identify itself unequivocally and for ever with just one type of strategy.[30] To be surprised because in the archipelago of Catholic ecclesiastical organizations, at least up to a point,[31] organizations and policies of opposing types co-exist would be tantamount to being surprised because in a certain institutional field there are companies which invest in one sector and others which do not, or do so in different directions.

Perhaps much sociology of religion and much theology still have to familiarize themselves with the decline of a certain idea of secularization which thinks that religion is destined to decline in modernization (or the decline of the opposite idea). Such a decline has taken place also and above all because, from the end of the nineteenth century,[32] the religious traditions 'of the church' and also of Catholicism have been far more complex and far more sophisticated than many theologians and many social analysts have supposed (cf. [c]).

5. The internal diversification of the religious contribution as one of the strategies of Catholic religious modernization (but not the only one)

With É. Poulat and R. Moro[33] we must get used to the fact that, at least in the case of Catholicism, the confrontation between modernization and religion has gradually taken the form of a confrontation between political, economic and scientific modernization on the one hand and religious modernization on the other; or that it has taken the form of a confrontation between religious modernization and social modernization as a confrontation between a part and the whole.

Moreover, as can be seen from many forms of political and economic modernization, we could also catalogue many forms of religious modernization (this has partly been done) and even forms of Catholic religious modernization. It is now clear that to these and other twentieth-century forms of Catholic religious modernization has been added a consistent modernization which provides a powerful ecclesiastical stimulus[34] to the internal diversification of what is on offer from the religions.[35] This type of Catholic religious modernization has certainly been prevalent in Italy and perhaps also in some other areas of Latin Europe dominated by Catholicism.

It is in the most recent phase of this strategy of internal diversification of what is on offer from religion which the Catholic Church practises, if not in 'mission lands', at least in the so-called 'Catholic monopolies' inserted into modernized social contexts characterized by protected religious markets,[36] that 'the movements' have become an important component. The majority of them originated and first spread[37] above all in Italy and Spain.

III. A first and partial response to the question

In the light of what has been said in the previous section I return to the three elements of implicit sociology contained in the question with which we are concerned.

On (a): In a highly differentiated social context (of society differentiated into functions, of organized systems differentiated from social systems, of social control differentiated from personal control, etc.) it is not useful to consider the church as a type of religious organization. And in fact that can no longer be established practically either in the study of the sociology of religion or in theoretical or empirical studies.

On (b): Even leaving out of account the usefulness and possibility of still talking of 'sects' in the classical sense of the term, in a socio-religious context like that of today it does not immediately make sense sociologically to speak of the 'sectarianization of the Catholic Church', since a simple opposition of church and sect can no longer be used for the analysis of religious organizations. It is now better to use them as concepts which do not exclude each other.

On (c): The permanence of a specialized social system in the function of religion and the role of leadership which some Christian traditions, certainly the Catholic tradition, are following in the formation of this reality at a global level also, compels the abandonment not only of the analytical 'church-sect' scheme but also of the classical and now over-simple idea of secularization as a progressive and inevitable decline of religion in the face of aggressive modernization and above all of the 'religion of the church'.

In short, Catholicism is committed in global society to playing an important role in the process of religious modernization. And it does so by all the main functional directives of the religious sub-system,[38] orientating itself on various types of specialized social systems in religion (social, organizational, interactive).

Conclusion

Obviously we could study how much, at what moments and in what sectors these forces take the form of deflationary policies, i.e. with marked analogies to the old phenomena of religious sectarianism, and how much, at what moments and in what sectors the opposite happens. Sociological judgment, which can also make a contribution, but to which the discernment of the gospel and the church certainly cannot be reduced, first of all sought to understand whether or not this or that religious policy increased the dominant position of the institutions and the Catholic organizations in the religious sub-system. At the moment, however, it seems impossible for sociology to maintain that a religious tradition of an ecclesial type must always, only and in any case resort to inflationary or 'liberal' policies, at the risk of otherwise showing itself the victim of a process of sectarian degeneration.

So in any attempt to understand the Catholic religious movements sociologically, and those which present the strongest and most indubitable analogies to sectarian experiences, it is not possible to leave out of account some features which are equally important, and certainly are not to be encountered in the classical sects. One need only think of the emphasis – going far beyond what is prescribed in the doctrine and canon law of the Catholic Church – on the relationship of reciprocal legitimation which each of these maintains with papal authority, or at least with the present pope. Given this, how would it ever be possible to speak of sects, when these movements base their autonomy from the local churches and their pastors on a special relationship with the pope, and are engaged in bitter rivalry with the territorial network of the Catholic 'supply side' of parishes and associations?[39] What has been observed of this phase (which is certainly not infinite) of the evolution of Catholic socio-religious forms is the transformation of the polity of the Catholic Church[40] from a model characterized by a mono-channel religious authority structure to a model characterized by a multi-channel religious authority structure.[41]

This response – a partial and initial one – to the question of the sectarianization of Catholicism is not meant to conclude the discussion simply by arguing that a certain interpretative hypothesis is inadequate. By offering a possible different interpretation of the same phenomenon it seeks to show that it fully shares many of the preoccupations that inspire the initial question. That religious fragmentation within the church has in many cases reached the point of raising the possibility of a real communication and co-responsibility between the faithful and groups of faithful within the church remains a clear and serious emergency, both pastoral and strategic. It remains true that the Catholic offer of religious participation allows many of the faithful less than a full experience of the church, which is often not even an approximation. Why otherwise would John Paul II have put on the list of serious failings of the church the inadequate reception of the event and the teaching of Vatican II (*Tertio Millennio Adveniente* no. 36), in awareness of which the church approached the recent Jubilee, a *mea culpa* in which is inserted an explicit reference to the inadequate welcome given to the invitation to ecclesiological renewal contained in *Lumen gentium*?

If, then, the main risk of Catholicism is not a priori that constituted by a certain number of manifestations of sectarianism, what is far more probable is the risk of growing complexity and growing socio-religious contingency, for example that contained in the individualization of the religious demand (which at root is essentially positive), giving rise to an immeasurable growth of internal religious pluralism and renouncing any sensed selectivity. For example, the currently prevalent abstention of the 'movements'[42] from ecclesial discernment could have crossed the threshold of prudent expectation of which the pastoral wisdom of the church has always been aware. Even before the sectarian character of the great part of these, the risk would be that of a tear in the fabric of the church that this abstention has allowed.[43] But the situation would be just as serious if, for example, the majority of the 'movements' did not have sectarian but 'liberal' features, as proved to be the case at some point immediately after the Council.

Finally, a phase of renewed discernment of religious pluralism within the church would bring with it the recovery of the awareness of a different weight of spiritual, ecclesiological and pastoral importance. This is the difference between 'ecclesial movement' and ecclesial association; between movements which constitute networks of ecclesial communities that tend completely to be pushed aside from the territorial networks of the ordinary ecclesial communities (inclusive and territorial: the dioceses and their parishes) and associations – the case of Catholic Action is a prominent one – through which the faithful help one another reciprocally to live out their baptism and their talents within the ordinary ecclesial communities which give them life.

Translated by John Bowden

Notes

1. Cf., to begin with, S. S. Acquaviva and E. Pace, *Sociologia delle religioni*, Rome 1992; L. Dani, 'Chiesa' in F. De Marchi, A. Ellena and B. Cattarinussi (eds), *Dizionario di sociologia*, Cinisello Balsamo 1987, pp. 342–50; W. H. Swatos, Jr, 'Monopolism, pluralism, acceptance, and reception: an integrated model for the church-sect theory', *Journal for the Scientific Study of Religion*, 1975, pp. 174–85 and id., 'Weber or Troeltsch ? Methodology, syndrome, and the development of church-sect theory', *Journal for the Scientific Study of Religion*, 1976, pp. 129–44.
2. For a synthetic framework cf. A. Favale (ed), *Movimenti ecclesiali contemporanei*, Rome 1991.
3. Cf. Acquaviva and Pace, *Sociologia* (n.1), pp. 119ff..
4. Cf. B. R. Wilson, 'Secularization: the inherited model' in P. Hammond (ed), *The Sacred and the Secular Age*, Berkeley 1985, pp. 9–20.
5. See 'Religious organization' in *Current Sociology* XXI/2, 1973, and 'Religious organization: a survey of some recent publications' in *Archives des sciences sociales des religions,* 1984, 1, pp. 83–102.
6. Cf.. F. X. Kaufmann, 'Religion et bureaucratie. Le probleme de l'organisation religieuse', *Social Compass* XXI/1, 1974, pp. 101–1 and 'The Church as a Religious Organization', *Concilium*, 1974/1, pp. 70–82.
7. Cf. R. J. Wuthnow, *Sociology of Religion* in N. J. Smelser (ed), *Handbook of Sociology*, Beverley Hills 1988, pp. 473–510.
8. Cf. B. R. Wilson, 'Religiosa, organizzazione' in *Enciclopedia delle scienze sociali*, VII, Rome 1997, pp. 381–95.
9. Cf. 'Religion and modernity in the French context: for a new approach to secularization', *Sociological Analysis*, 1990, S15–S25.
10. *Funktion der Religion*, Frankfurt am Main 1977, and *Die Religion der Gesellschaft*, Frankfurt am Main 2000.
11. For the most inclusive synthesis cf. *Soziale Systeme*, Frankfurt am Main 1984.
12. Cf. 'Modernità e differenziazione sociale' in N. Luhmann et al., *Moderno postmoderno*, Milano 1987, pp. 88–97.

13. See e.g. N. Luhmann, *Die Gesellschaft der Gesellschaft*, Frankfurt 1997, pp. 159ff.
14. For a deeper treatment relating of the themes relating to the concept of 'functional differentiation' cf. especially Niklas Luhmann, *Soziologische Aufklärung 4. Beiträge zur funktionalen Differenzierung der Gesellschaft*, Opladen 1987, and id. (ed), *Soziale Differenzierung. Zur Geschichte einer Idee*, Opladen 1985.
15. Cf. N. Luhmann and R. de Giorgi, *Teoria della società*, Milan 1992, pp. 302ff.
16. *La differenziazione sociale*, Bari and Rome 1982.
17. Cf. Luhmann, *Funktion der Religion* (n. 10), pp. 30ff.
18. See C. Baraldi, G. Corsi and E. Esposito, *Glossario dei termini della teoria dei sistemi di Niklas Luhmann*, Urbino 1990, pp. 122ff.
19. Cf. S. Cassese, *La crisi dello Stato*, Rome and Bari 2002, and *Lo Stato introvabile*, Rome 1997, which also provides the richest information.
20. Cf. N. Luhmann, *Organisation und Entscheidung*, Opladen 2000.
21. Cf. Luhmann, *Funktion der Religion* (n.10), pp. 284ff; id., *Die Religion der Gesellschaft* (n.10), pp. 226ff..
22. Cf. Luhmann, *Die Religion der Gesellschaft* (n.10), pp. 380ff., and id., *Funktion der Religion* (n.10), pp. 72ff. Cf. also Baraldi, Corsi and Esposito, *Glossario* (n.18), pp. 134ff.
23. When, finally, I indicate the specific character of ecclesial associationism and thus of Catholic Action in particular as a very interesting topic, one might also consider the question of the 'religious choice' of the ACI as a specific product of the reception of Vatican II. For a splendid presentation of the 'religious choice' cf. C. M. Martini, *La Parola nella città*, Bologna 1984, pp. 235–36.
24. Cf. W Pannenberg and N. Luhmann, 'Die Allegemeingültigkeit der Religion', *Evangelische Kommentare* 11, 1978, pp. 350–57.
25. Cf. K. Rahner, *Considerazioni teologiche sulla secolarizzazione*, Rome 1969, and H.U von Balthasar, *Abbattere i bastioni*, Turin 1966, on the impact on the church of social transformations. These still deserve careful reading today, perhaps even more than when they were written.
26. A thread of research which could show the different capacities of the various religious traditions to bring together the specific characteristics of social phenomenon focusses on the political, ecumenical and inter-religious dimensions and even the success of Catholics by comparison with the inadequate approach of other inter-church and inter-religious organizations. Cf. F. Teixiera, 'The Paradigm of Assisi', *Concilium* 2001/3, pp. 111–20; L. Diotallevi, 'E' la globalizzazione delle fedi', *Corriere dell'Umbria*, 24 January 2002, p. 19, a special insert devoted to the encounter of many religions at Assisi, with contributions by W. Kasper, M. Nour Dachan, F. Lotti, A. Papisca, R. Prodi. K. Annan, V. Coli, E. Fortunato, S. Goretti, G. Chiaretti, D. Aristei, V. Paglia, L. Diotallevi and others; P. Beyer, 'Globalizing systems, global culture models and religion(s)', *International Sociology*, 1998, 1, pp. 79–94, and 'The religious system

of global society: a sociological look at contemporary religion and religions', *Numen* 45, 1998, pp. 1–29.

27. Luhmann, *Funktion der Religion* (n. 10), p. 56.

28. Cf. Swatos, 'Monopolism' and 'Weber or Troeltsch?' (n. 1).

29. Cf. J. A. Beckford, *Religione e società industriale avanzata*, Rome 1991.

30. Cf. N. Luhmann, 'Society, Meaning, Religion – Based on Self-Reference', *Sociological Analysis* 46, 1985, pp. 5–20, also from this perspective a very important text.

31. Perhaps the most important part of an analysis begins with an evaluation of the relations between this threshold and the demands of the gospel; it is certainly difficult to legitimate the daring pastoral and disciplinary opportunisms to those who often regard themselves as spectators.

32. See R. Moro, 'Il "modernismo buono"', *Storia contemporanea* 4, 1988, pp. 625–716.

33. Cf. also F. X. Kaufmann and A. Zingerle (eds), *Vatikanum II und Modernisierung*, Paderborn, Munich, Vienna and Zurich 1986.

34. The history of this policy covers the whole of the nineteenth century in Italy (cf. Diotallevi 1999, *Religione, chiesa* and 2001, *Il rompicapo*). For a symbolic recent example see E. Pace, 'Rivoluzione nel personale, restaurazione nel politico. Neopentecostali e riaggregazione cattolica' in G. Guizzardi (ed), *L'organizzazione dell'eterno*, Milan 1984, 196–221.

35. Not to be confused with the model of the 'pillars'. See L. Diotallevi, 'Internal Competition in a National Religious Monopoly: The Catholic Effect and the Italian Case', *Sociology of Religion* 63/2, 2002, pp. 137–56, and also G. Donnadieu, 'Vers un marché du religieux?', *Futuribles* 260, 2001, pp. 5–21, and R. Della Cava, 'Vatican Policy: 1978–1990: an updated overview', *Social Research* 59, 1992, pp. 169–99.

36. I have tried to offer some reasons in my 'Verso una denominazionalizzazione del cattolicesimo italiano?', *Religioni e Società*, 2001, pp. 40–41. With reference to the solution adopted by Opus Dei it would probably be better to speak of 'prelaturization'.

37. Cf. Favale (ed), *Movimenti ecclesiali* (n. 2) and also *L'Osservatore Romano*, 28 May 1998 and 1–2 June 1998, with the list of officials invited to a kind of world encounter of officially recognized Catholic 'movements'.

38. Cf. Luhmann, *Funktion der Religion* (n.10), pp. 54 ff.

39. Cf. Diotallevi , 'Verso una denominazionalizzazione' (n. 36).

40. For the concept of 'religious polity' cf. M. McMullen, 'Religious polities as institutions', *Social forces* 73/2, 1994, pp. 709–28.

41. Cf. Diotallevi 2001, *Il rompicapo*, pp.102ff., and 'Internal competition' (n. 35), pp. 149ff..

42. Not without exceptions. One might think of speeches by the bishops of Foligno (11 August 1995), Florence (25 March 1995), Turin (28 May 1995), Palermo

(22 February 1996), Puglia (1 December 1996), and Vicenza (18 December 1996). For a synthesis of the themes most often dealt with cf. 'Le norme e l'implicito', *Il Regno* 8/1996, p. 205. Cf. also the speech by Cardinal C. M. Martini at the synod on the 'laity' in 1997, published in *Il Regno* 21, 1997, 666 (but see already *Il Regno* 14, 1986, pp. 361–62).

43. One might think of the lowest level of reception, for example in various areas of central and southern Italy, of the recommendation on the celebration of festive masses contained in no. 36 of John Paul II's *Dies Domini*.

Dissidence and Conformism in Religious Movements: What Difference Separates the Catholic Charismatic Renewal and Pentecostal Churches?

DAVID LEHMANN

This article tries to distinguish between religious movements which transform religious life and others which do so to a small or insignificant extent, using the contrast between conformism and dissidence – and emphatically avoiding quasi-political metaphors such as 'progressive' and conservative'. In outlining the contrast, drawing principally on Brazilian and North American examples, the article relies on the dialectic between popular and erudite religion, and compares the Charismatic Renewal movement within Catholicism with the Pentecostal movement in search of significant differences, or rather in search of how to understand the differences and the similarities.

I. Religious institutions are always vulnerable to pressure from below

The religious field, which to some may appear deeply conservative, is in fact in permanent flux. Indeed, against certain sorts of expectation, religious institutions seem remarkably open – some might say, vulnerable – to external pressure for change. Compared with political institutions, for example, they are less able, and on occasion have less desire, to resist the voices of the disempowered, the poor or simply of their rank-and-file followers. The space for change, and for the laity to be a protagonist of change, is most self-evident in secularized societies where the state has detached itself from formal links with the institution of religion, or where, as in the UK, those formal links have lost their compulsory content[1] with regard to observance of religious norms. But even in countries – many Muslim countries apart from Turkey, as well as in Israel – where the links between state and religion are formal and carry some degree of coercive force, the institutions, doctrines and practices of religious life do not stand still, and are subject to multiple pressures from 'below'. The same could even be said of the Catholic Church. For if the church has, in the opinion of many, resisted and repulsed what the hierarchy perceived as a threat from the 'People's Church' tendency and certain versions of liberation theology, it has in contrast tolerated, and more recently even encouraged, charismatic manifestations which a few decades ago were viewed with much suspicion by all save its sponsor the late Cardinal Suenens.

1. Myth of origin

The Charismatic Renewal is a tendency, perhaps even a movement, which counts itself within Catholicism and which, after some hesitation and various prior stages, received official recognition from the Vatican in September 1993.[2] Its standard history, or myth of origin, dates its birth quite precisely to a prayer weekend at Duquesne University in Pittsburgh in 1967. (Pentecostals too have a precise date of birth at Azusa Street in Los Angeles in 1906.) From there a package of practices circulated among groups of Catholics throughout the world which uncannily replicate Pentecostal practices. These are, principally, healing; speaking in tongues; deliverance/exorcism; group prayer meetings under tight lay leadership; invocation and recognition of the concrete objective presence of the Holy Spirit in people's lives and in prayer meetings; hostility to the permissive society; modesty in dress; male leadership; the central place accorded to a conversion experience. The Charismatics' relationship with the hierarchy was managed at first by Cardinal Suenens (who retired in the mid-1980s) who continues to be regarded as their father figure and sponsor. Suenens' seems to have played a careful diplomatic role, sometimes espousing the language of the charismatics wholeheartedly and sometimes seeking to relativize their position in a liberal direction.[3] Priestly supervision of charismatics is variable, as is charismatic obedience of or search for it, but although one should not expect an absolutely standard package, it is surprising how much coincidence there is among monographic studies at least in the USA.[4] The reason for this consistency, which is also observed among the highly decentralized Pentecostals, lies not in uniformity of direction or doctrine, but in their common relationship to a concept of frontier: a community is born again, sets itself apart, and then places much power in the hands of a leader. The group meets frequently at fixed hours (thus setting their lifestyle apart); it develops distinctive modes of dress; it regulates members' lives in innumerable very detailed ways.[5] This emerges from the case studies and also fits with North American Pentecostalism, although it is impossible to know how representative the cases are . In South America, less contaminated by Puritan traditions, discipline seems to be less fierce, although we lack the detailed case studies.

2. A middle class phenomenon

It is usually accepted that, in contrast to the People's Church tendency, the Charismatic renewal is a middle-class phenomenon, but this needs some qualification, even if technically accurate. The same, after all, could be said, and demonstrated, with statistical observations, about the Catholic Church as a whole in Latin America.[6] Middle class may not mean 'establishment' or élite, especially in the United States. In the case studies already mentioned of the Renewal, followers are of middle-class status, but they are not bearers of a heritage of thought or power.[7] Chesnut's review of a wide range of sources, though not statistical ones, indicates that in Latin America the Charismatic Renewal is acquiring a steadily more 'popular' following and losing some of its middle-class bias. Furthermore, and although it might be controversial or disappointing in some quarters to say so, if we look at the social composition and the numbers of its followers in Latin America the Charismatic Renewal merits far more the description of a movement 'from below' (though not precisely 'from the poor'), than the People's Church, which in the final analysis is more a tendency within the world of religious professionals and activists.[8] On this argument, therefore, 'even' the Catholic Church is receptive to pressures from below.

That word 'below' has many connotations, and they reflect variations in religious culture, political culture, and theology. For some it might refer to the laity in general, for others to the poor and disinherited, and for yet others to the unlettered. Beyond the realm of the faithful, no religious movement or institution – least of all those with a history of dominance in secularized societies – can ignore pressure either from the media or from the mass of non-observant people who, though they may never set foot in a synagogue, church or mosque, still look to the institution of religion as important and expect religious professionals to observe certain standards of behaviour. This is what Grace Davie calls 'vicarious religion'.[9] Whatever the precise connotation of the word 'below', the institutions of religion have demonstrated that they can absorb these pressures and survive, without resorting to coercion, to a monopoly on any real political or resource, or indeed in most settings even to a monopoly of salvation and the felicity associated with it. Proponents of the 'rational choice approach', or economic theory of religion, even claim that *less* religious monopoly of itself brings *more* religious participation[10] and point to the US as an illustration of this idea. That may well be an example of how ideological enthusiasm can convert an intelligent insight into an exaggerated (and ethnocentric) claim: nevertheless it is clear that even tired or rigid – or *apparently* rigid – religious monopolies or quasi-monopolies (as in Latin America) still have to respond to pressure from below and from without.

II. The popular and the erudite in religious culture

One reason why even the most 'monolithic' religions change, yet remain in so many ways the same, is the permanent tension between the popular and the erudite within the religious sphere. It is a tension which is never resolved and can never be resolved. Religion is an activity sanctioned by an idea that 'it was always so', just as ritual, without which religion is literally unthinkable, can be defined as an activity which occurs at fixed or pre-ordained moments of an endlessly repeated cycle of years, months, weeks or days. Yet how can the audience, the public, the potential followers or faithful, the laity, be convinced that 'it was always so'? The answer is not that they are convinced by erudite disquisitions marshalling archaeological and other scientific evidence, let alone by theology. Rather they have minds in which certain sequences and certain symbolic evocations seem to have evolved to infer longevity of practices from their symbolic structure. Pascal Boyer describes the resemblance between the fears and motivations driving ritual 'scripts', and the fears and motivations observable in people suffering from obsessive-compulsive disorder. From this he concludes that since rituals allude to 'precautions against undetectable hazards' they are highly 'attention-grabbing' and 'people feel emotionally bound to perform them in the right way'.[11] Analogously, one can imagine how certain combinations of images and symbols can endow a performance with the authority of longevity and authenticity. Take the following imaginary example: if I stand in front of the Duomo in Florence and announce that those who ride their bicycles will be guaranteed eternal happiness, I will attract no attention. Passers-by will be unable to make sense of what I am doing. But if I grow a long white beard and proclaim, in a singsong voice, and repeatedly, 'Repent for the end

of the world is nigh', people will at least know what I am talking about. If I
brandish a black leather-bound book and describe in a prophetic voice how
people might change their lives for ever by pronouncing a few words ('He
died that you might be saved!') concerning a prophet said to have lived 2000
years ago, I may even convert some tourists. Indeed, the Jewish Chabad sect
have set up offices in the Venice Ghetto where they do precisely that:
dressed in their unmistakably Chassidic garb, they accost pensive (and self-
evidently Jewish) tourists as the sun goes down, in a square littered with
Holocaust memorials, and draw them into a discussion about their roots,
their origins and their Jewishness. (Success rates in bringing the tourists
'back' to religious observance are unrecorded.)

If religion is legitimated, *inter alia*, by such choreographed invocations of
historical roots, then evidently a monopoly of access to the supernatural is
impossible to protect, rendering religious officialdom (erudite religion) constantly vulnerable to discredit. In America, the discredit and relegitimation
process is fuelled by schismatic proliferation and migration of followers
between churches, whereby preachers and pastors break away from their
churches of origin and try their luck in the marketplace. In Latin American
Catholicism, and in Latin Europe, the place of schismatic proliferation is
taken by popular religion: a promiscuous mixture of ritual devices and symbolic allusions which wriggles out of doctrinal or ritual orthodoxy without
ever going so far as to defy it. Examples could fill many encyclopaedias. The
cult of the Virgin of Guadalupe, the cult of Padre Pío, and the renewed
proliferation of pilgrimages, mostly to sites of miraculous appearances of the
Virgin Mary, all illustrate the vitality of a religiosity which escapes the direct
control of the hierarchy. We also know, in the cases of Guadalupe and of
Padre Pío, how the hierarchy has shifted position under pressure from the
laity: the recent canonization of the *indio* who is said to have had the vision of
the Virgin of Guadalupe in 1536, Juan Diego, has taken place in the face of
opposition from scholars who reasoned that there is no evidence that he
ever existed, and it is well known that Padre Pio's stigmata were viewed
with much scepticism by the Vatican for a long time, until the pressure of
the mass support for him and his works became irresistible. Indeed, the
tidal wave of canonizations by John Paul II demonstrates his apparent conviction that the revivification of the church must pass through a more formal
recognition of the reality of popular religion than his recent predecessors
were prepared to accord. It is reminiscent of the priests who scoured
Northern Europe in the wake of the Reformation searching for saintly
remains, which were then transported, for example, to Spain and used to

'officialize' feasts and saint's days so as to impose some degree of order on local religious life.[12]

III. Religious movements and their conceptualization

Religious movements mobilize collectivities in the name of changing the mechanisms of reproduction of particular 'religions', just as social movements in general change the mechanisms of reproduction of the social, economic and political order.[13] (By a particular religion is meant here a set of interlocking ritual practices with an identity, a name, and an institutional expression.) In other words they do not invent a doctrine or liturgy *de novo*, but propagate changes in those religious institutions which exist, in the name of origins, roots, the 'true faith'. To achieve change, though, they have to engage with the mercurial and dialectic relationship between the popular and the erudite or official versions. Religious movements – understood as mobilizing non-officialdom, or in Catholic terms, the laity – must therefore involve a change in the relationship between the popular and erudite forms, rather than a change in the one or the other.

1. Catholic 'basismo'

In Latin America one candidate for the status of religious movement might be the 'People's Church' tendency (*Iglesia Popular* – *Igreja Popular* in Portuguese), most in evidence in Brazil during the era of dictatorship and democratic transition, and in Central America's period of civil wars which lasted from (at least) 1975 to the early 1990s. It is not coterminous with liberation theology, which has now given birth to many tendencies of its own, and whose most distinguished exponent, Gustavo Gutiérrez, has kept his distance from any engagement with issues of church structure. Born out of a diversity of influences from European Catholic movements in the inter-war and early post-war periods – the social doctrine, the worker-priests of France, Azione Catolica, Christian Democracy – and above all Vatican II and Liberation Theology, the People's Church consists of a diversity of local groups guided by theologians and activists and linked to the church through the 'Pastorais'[14] or ministries catering to the Landless, to Urban Youth, to Women, and other social groups depending on local priorities. At its heart are the activists employed by these organizations and priests and bishops linked to them in various capacities. The activists are in the role of educators – of whom the first were the *promotores* who applied Paulo Freire's ideas about popular education in rural areas. The *base* or grass roots, are the nucleus of a popular intelligentsia, taking a student-like role in base communities (*comunidades de base*), discussion groups and seminars. This movement certainly provided leadership for urban movements of revindication and collective consumption,[15] and they were hotbeds of discussion about how the church itself should change, sometimes supporting the theologian and proponent of radical structural change in the church, Leonardo Boff[16] in the days when he was in conflict with the hierarchy and before he left the priesthood to become an ecological activist. So Catholic *basismo*, as I have termed it,[17] has been influential: it provided the cadres of urban mobilization and in Brazil of Lula's Workers' Party (founded in 1979); it provided the beginnings of a philosophy of action for the NGOs which were burgeoning during the dark days of authoritarianism in the 1970s and since then have taken their place in the international development community worldwide. But on the ground, since the late 1980s or early 1990s, observers, and even activists themselves, have been overcome by a sense of retreat or loss. They look back nostalgically to a period, which lasted no more than a decade, during which the triple struggle for human rights, against 'savage capitalism' and for change in the church itself, commanded a high international profile and widespread legitimacy.

2. Religious movement or sub-culture?

It seems a little cruel to deny to liberation theology and the People's Church the title of religious movement, because they have made such a notable contribution to theology, to the life of the church, to international civil society, to social movements in Latin America and to international development philosophies. Such has been their influence that even those who oppose them have borrowed ideas and methods from them – as witness the production of a 'sanitized' liberation theology by the Vatican in the 1980s and the pope's renewed emphasis on the 'preferential option for the poor' after 1989.

But this is not a properly religious movement, precisely because of its approach to popular religion. Liberation theology, as part of the modernism associated with Vatican II, first opposed popular religion as a type of superstition and false consciousness. Later many of its protagonists changed their views, but their approach remained too intellectual, they reified and idealized popular religion, so making a theory of it and interrupting the epidemiological patterns of its spread. So we are faced here not so much with a movement as with a sub-culture, best described by the French word *mouvance*, evoking networks, atmosphere, shared meanings, but not pro-active multi-levelled interventions producing social change. If they contributed to change it was through their influence beyond the religious field, as I have described.

If liberation theology led to more change outside the church than within, to more change in political culture than in religious culture, the opposite might be true of other movements such as Communione e Liberazione, Schoenstadt, the Foccolari, and the Charismatic Renewal. Although these have enjoyed a wider mass base and a less complicated affinity with popular religious devotion, they have not developed a project, or promoted the social forces, which are associated with a social movement engaged in the redirection of society or of a major institution such as the church. Opus Dei has a project, but it does not have a mass base or promote social forces; CL had, and the Charismatic Renewal has, the social base, but their projects are of transformation of individuals, not of the institution or of society. (CL, it must be said, committed a similar mistake to the People's Church – throwing its lot in with a political cause, namely the Italian Christian Democratic Party, and one which disintegrated in spectacular fashion.) They are regarded by many as 'conservative', though to affix that label to them is as misleading as to affix the label of 'progressive' to movements inspired by the social doctrine and liberation theology. Such labels, drawn from everyday political vocabulary, ignore the specifically religious dimension of religious movements and treat them as if they were political factions.

IV. Dissidence and conformism in religious movements: Charismatic Renewal versus Pentecostalism

It would make better sense, since we are discussing religious movements and not political parties, to think of their *cultural dissidence* or their *cultural conformism* (rather than conservatism). The axis from dissidence to conformism concerns the extent to which, through ritual and symbolic enactments, including choreography of public occasions, for example, movements conform to or depart from the habits and traditions conventionally consecrated by hegemonic élites or prevailing structures of power.

1. Political conformism

For example: the Brazilian Universal Church of the Kingdom of God – usually described as neo-Pentecostal because it has innovated in so many ways – has adopted the method of spectacularization, has built its own cathedrals, proclaims unabashedly the millions of dollars it receives from its followers in tithes and donations, and generally offends the intellectual élite and the guardians of media power.[18] (Interestingly, though, its phenomenal popular success has eventually led politicians to befriend it rather than denigrate it as they used to until the late 1990s). This is *cultural* dissidence on a large scale, but hardly *political* dissidence. Conversely, the People's Church, though politically radical, was culturally conformist – adopting the method of studying to improve one's politics, and remaining highly dependent on bishops and priests for its viability. The dissidence of the Universal Church is accentuated by the way it builds on symbols associated with the Catholic Church and longer-established Pentecostal churches: the use of 'offerings' or 'requests to Jesus' written on pieces of paper and handed to the pastor, like votive offerings; the use of 'holy oil' to 'anoint' people; the use of terms like 'bishop' and 'cathedral' which no other Pentecostal church uses – and which the Brazilian press always puts in inverted commas. These devices are close enough to Catholicism to evoke a sacred association, but deviant enough to shock, on account of their use by a challenger for Catholicism's unique place in the imaginary ordering of society and state.

Devotional movements like Schoenstadt and the Foccolari are conformist because they look for a niche within the established order, and campaign to bring people to themselves and their own styles of devotion. They are not locally rooted, operating rather in transnational networks, and do not exhibit the mercurial adaptability of popular religion. They are highly specialized in particular activities – sometimes charitable, like the 'Legionarios de Cristo', sometimes just creating new spaces and encouraging followers to meet and pray together – and append themselves to one or another fragment of the church's multifarious apparatus.

2. Charismatic Renewal: between dissidence and conformism

The Charismatic Renewal, though, presents a test case which may enable us to draw the line between dissidence and conformism. On the face of it, the wildfire spread of this movement has definitively blurred the boundaries: like Pentecostals, Charismatics receive the gift of the Holy Spirit, speak in tongues, and practise public healing by the Spirit. Written black on white, so to speak, it is hard to distinguish them from Pentecostals. Charismatic groups – with evangelical-sounding names like 'Maranata', 'Sword of the Spirit', 'Word of God', 'Precious Blood'[19] – meet in churches, but (apart from the mass itself) their celebrations do not follow a liturgical formula, and are led by lay people trained in courses and seminars. In Bahia, Brazil, I was told that so long as they meet in the church, the hierarchy feels comfortable with them[20] – but the case studies in the US reveal a wide variation in degrees of hierarchical control: Csordas describes cases (from the 1970s through to the early 1990s) in which local leaderships developed ever tighter regimentation over the private lives of small groups of followers, while elaborating ritual performance, especially rituals separating the community from 'the world', in ever more minute detail,[21] and how these tendencies were moderated by a combination of internal and hierarchical intervention. Both Csordas and McGuire describe mechanisms of certification and confirmation of charisms, especially prophecy, which disempower rank and file participants and empower local leaders.[22] These are all to be found, in varying degrees, in Pentecostal churches – as are situations of a different kind, where prophecy runs riot (at a cost to institutional stability). McGuire[23] describes some differences relating to loyalty towards the hierarchy and the encouragement of emotionalism, but given that these differences are few and subject to wide variation in local practice, their significance is open to doubt.

Although one might have expected the Charismatic Renewal to spawn breakaway moves by local leaders itching to become independent of the hierarchy and the mainstream, reports of such things are very rare. On the contrary, field observation in Brazil (in 2002), for example, reveals that the mainstream is becoming 'infected' by the capillary spread of charismatic practices such as swaying of hands and cries of 'Hallelujah!'.[24] Also, the Charismatic Renewal, not to be outdone by the Pentecostals, with whom it is in more direct competition than the hierarchy itself, is adopting the spectacularization hitherto associated with the Universal Church.[25] Certain priests in Brazil – and perhaps elsewhere – are becoming media stars – like Padre Marcelo Rossi of São Paulo, who fills football stadiums with crowds of singing enthusiasts, and makes best-selling CDs in which religious words are set to 'pop' music.

3. Pentecostalism: independent from hierarchy

At the grassroots, Pentecostalism appears so different from mainstream Catholicism that Pentecostals in Brazil refer to themselves as 'Christians' but to Catholics as 'not Christian but Catholics' – though this may merely reflect nothing more than their own lack of a religious upbringing. Catholicism – in both its popular and its erudite expressions – depends heavily on the existence of a hierarchy, and that hierarchy attaches great importance to elaborate intellectual structures produced by generations of theologians and 'clercs de l'Eglise'. The popular may be indifferent to their learning, but in Catholicism the existence and the authority of the hierarchy is an integral component of popular religious life, which the bishops and priests may not have formulated, but which they do bless and legitimate though their presence in local celebrations of all kinds. Pentecostal churches do not have a hierarchy in the same sense, with doctrinal prerogatives and ceremonial paraphernalia, and although the larger ones, such as the Assemblies of God or the Four-Square Gospel Church, do have modern, often highly centralized, apparatuses, these are largely concerned with administrative matters. They are not global bureaucracies, but operate at local or regional level – so in Brazil the Assemblies have totally autonomous State Conventions in each of the country's 26 states, with only a decorative national structure.[26] So long as followers of the Charismatic Renewal remain loyal to the hierarchy, perhaps the difference separating them from the Pentecostals will be clear. This, however, depends on the hierarchy's response: it may remain uninvolved – as to some extent seems to be the case in North America – or it can look to the renewal as an ally and an evangelizing movement, as seems to be the case in Latin America, where the practice of holding mass meetings gives bishops a chance to demonstrate their support for the movement. The figures propagated by the head office of the International Catholic Charismatic Services in Rome, if reliable, certainly make the movement seem a valuable ally: they show 73 million Catholics in the Charismatic Renewal in Latin America (16% of the total) and 10 million (14% of the total) in North America.[27] But the significance of these figures must vary enormously between North and South: in the USA mass meetings for charismatics tend to be run by non-Catholic Pentecostal and Evangelical organizations whereas in Latin America the 'tribal' frontier between the Renewal and the Pentecostals is clearly drawn both locally and in staged mass public events.[28]

An illustration of the extent to which the episcopate can control and even use the Charismatic Renewal for its institutional purposes is found in

Guadalajara – Mexico's premier diocese, with a reputation for great devotion, and where 32% of the country's training centres for priests and religious are to be found, as well as an estimated 150,000 active lay participants in Catholic organizations and movements.[29] Here, by the 1980s, the episcopate was somewhat taken aback by the rapid growth and above all the autonomy of the Charismatic Renewal, especially with respect to 'ecstatic demonstrations . . . the miraculous and extraordinary nature of their rituals, and . . . . the recognition of charisms'.[30] It seems that only in the early stages, in the 1970s, had the Guadalajara Renewal participated in assemblies with Pentecostals and Evangelicals, but still the hierarchy took the situation in hand in the mid-1980s, and proceeded, despite some resistance, to 'standardize and bureaucratize', 'exercising institutional control over the charismatic power developed by lay people who questioned and threatened the specialized, hierarchical order of the church'. It remains to be seen whether this pattern of conflict and co-optation prevails throughout the region, or whether deeper rifts will appear. De la Torre sees this as one of many instances demonstrating the 'transversal' nature of a Catholic Church which is highly permeable, as I said at the outset, to influences from without.

We have for long been aware that it would be mistaken to believe that a 'progressive' post-Conciliar message, emphasizing the struggle against 'structural sin' and institutionalized violence, and advocating the preferential option for the poor, has a special attraction for poor people, just as we know that the high proportion of dispossessed among Pentecostals does not make them progressive in political outlook. The individualism of the Charismatic Renewal is not necessarily a symptom of a bias towards certain socio-economic groups, but may reflect rather its appeal, like that of the Pentecostals, to people with two characteristics: those who, though nominally Catholic, have had almost no religious formation at all, independent of their socio-economic status, and those who have no connection with local popular religion and so find one in these more synthetic (but no less real) communities. In this connection the account by Csordas[31] of an attempt to relocate followers and make them live in close communities is instructive. The project did not succeed in creating a physical community out of disparate multi-generation households.

These brief remarks do not enable us to draw a clear line of distinction between Pentecostals and the Charismatic Renewal. The ritual routines which mark their time cycles and the boundaries of their community, and the symbolic apparatus which accompanies them are too similar. What then of the erudite aspect?

V. Movements of religious transformation and the role of the erudite

The erudite aspect enables a religion to build and perpetuate a tradition. Re-enactment of tradition, the successful and legitimate invocation of tradition, contributes to the creation of the imaginary universal community to which local religious practices must relate if they are to be anything other than contingent and ephemeral gatherings, and indeed if their performances are to carry any meaning. If you ask a *mãe de santo* – a priestess in a Brazilian possession cult – what is the *meaning* of rituals she performs, she will not understand the question. She may be able to state their *purpose* and their *motive* but not their meaning. (Interestingly, since French anthropologists – notably Roger Bastide – developed a theory on their behalf of their African origins, these practitioners have tried to identify themselves in terms of faithfulness to a tradition[32] and have even tried to create an institution which would define an orthodoxy.[33]) So her religious practices cannot be a movement, endowed with a project of transformation of either the religious institution or of the world. Likewise, popular religion is not capable of transforming religion or society, and the Charismatic Renewal likewise. It is not by accident that when Pascal Boyer's book reaches the theme of institutionalized religion he abandons the cognitive and evolutionary approaches which he has used to explain why we engage in ritual and why we believe in spirits, and adopts an institutional rational-choice approach in which religion is a strategic institution, pursuing political aims in the broad sense of the word, and thus requiring doctrines and an intellectual apparatus.

Now a movement is something which brings about major change – in the institutions and culture of a religion, or in a society, or sometimes both. But to bring about change a project of transformation is needed, and this is what the Renewal lacks, and it explains why despite their millions of followers, they have had fewer historical consequences than the small band of the People's Church and liberation theology. World religions have doctrines which define the meaning of their core rituals. These may not define what the rituals signify in practice to most of their followers most of the time, but they do contribute to the institutional project, and the institutional project has real historical consequences. Religious change therefore involves firstly changing or conceivably replacing tradition-bearing institutions, and thus conferring legitimacy on the new which is presented as a better version of the old. But religious change also means rearranging the relationship between these institutions, with their universal vocation, and the popular, with its local roots.

The Charismatic Renewal remains within the realm of the popular. It does not propound change in erudite Catholicism, or in the institutions or doctrines of the church. It remains within the church both physically and metaphorically. Even the most mediatic padre is still a padre, linked to the hierarchy. Obviously, the crowd-pulling performances of the singing priests have made some bishops uneasy, but that unease is rapidly dissipated by the sight of the crowds they attract. The Renewal therefore could be seen as an addition to Catholicism's repertoire of popular religion, adapted to a more global context and to a highly secularized laity possessing almost zero religious formation, but sharing the cultural conformism of popular religion generally.

Now, in posing the same question of Pentecostalism in Latin America, we can see the relevance of the links between the Pentecostal imaginary and indigenous religion and possession cults (in Brazil and Africa). Pentecostalism clearly represents a cultural dissidence – and this can hardly be due to any explicit political message – a message which, in so far as it exists, is broadly conservative and rarely explicitly formulated. Rather the Pentecostal claim to dissidence is due to their redrawing of boundaries both between traditions and also between the popular and the erudite. Pentecostals clearly and loudly distance themselves from Catholic popular religion – regarding patron saints and pilgrimages as a type of idolatry. They also have a very different relationship with possession cults in both Brazil and Africa.[34] Catholicism for its part has a history of co-existence with the cults, at least in Brazil, occasionally denouncing them as 'paganism', but more usually turning a blind eye. Pentecostals, however, while denouncing the cults comprehensively as paganism and the work of the devil, give much credence to their efficacy and borrow much symbolism and imagery from them, above all ideas of possession and of forces of evil, and of the ever-present threat to the integrity of our persons posed by those forces and by those who are in league with them. This is not just verbal denunciation: it involves symbolic identification of possession cults with the devil and pervasive practice of rituals of deliverance (a word I prefer to exorcism because of the routine, almost perfunctory, character the ritual has acquired among the Pentecostals). This emphasis on the devil, on the forces of darkness, the *maligno* etc. is especially prominent in neo-Pentecostal churches, but the same applies to Pentecostals generally, except that they tend to evoke the forces of evil with more discretion.

Conclusion: the same on paper, but different in spirit

The case studies of the Charismatic Renewal in the USA certainly show close affinity with Pentecostalism in the USA. The texts read and sung by followers of the Charismatic Renewal in Latin America also show close affinity with Pentecostal texts. But when we place these movements in the public sphere and in relation to the popular erudite dialectic, and also when we place them in the context of Catholicism's informal monopoly, we can see that in Latin America Pentecostalism is a cultural dissidence, while the Charismatic Renewal is not. It should however be noted that cultural dissidence is not social or religious transformation: whether Pentecostalism can achieve that is another question.

Notes

1. The United Kingdom has a unique regime in which the Church of England is the 'established' church with the monarch as its formal head, yet the church has no secular power and no religious monopoly.

2. The precise situation is that on 30 November 1990 the Pontifical Council for the Laity granted recognition to the Catholic Fraternity of Charismatic Covenant Communities and Fellowships and then in 1993 it recognized the International Catholic Charismatic Service (ICCRS) 'as a body for the promotion of the Catholic Charismatic Renewal'. This body has its seat in Rome and its president is elected by its Council from nominations approved by the Pontifical Council for the Laity. The ICCRS is the successor to a body first established in 1978 in Brussels by Cardinal Suenens.

3. Thus in the authoritative Malines Document I (1974), written largely by Killian McDonnell under Suenens' supervision and sponsorship, there are numerous warnings against excesses, against 'fundamentalism' in the interpretation of the Bible (V.C), against 'demonomania' or the obsession with evil spirits (VI.H) – even while the documents recognize that the Bible should be read – and that evil is a real force in the world. Prophecy is described a maturing process, and when necessary should be 'submitted to the discernment of a Bishop' (VI.G) These are all central enthusiasms of the Charismatics, as case studies repeatedly demonstrate, yet the movement's main sponsor is clearly seeking either to domesticate them or to portray a 'moderate' face to the outside world. Malines II (1978) follows a similar path and Malines III (1978) is a set of parallel texts by Cardinal Suenens and one of the most prominent voices of Latin America's voiceless, Archbishop Helder Camara of Recife and Olinda in Brazil. K. McDonnell (ed), *Presence, Power and Praise: Documents on the Charismatic Renewal*, Collegeville, Minnesota: The Liturgical Press 1980.

4. Basic monographic case studies for the Charismatic Renewal in the USA are:

M. McGuire, *Pentecostal Catholics: Power, Charisma and Order in a Religious Movement*, Philadelphia: Temple University Press 1982; M. J. Neitz, *Charisma and Community: A Study of Religious Commitment within the Charismatic Renewal*, New Brunswick: Transaction Books 1987; T. Csordas, *Language, Charisma and Creativity*, Berkeley: University of California Press 1997.

5. This is much in evidence in the studies by McGuire and by Csordas (n. 4). Csordas (p.128) describes the disciplines of one community and also of the 'Training Course' which at one time its followers attended (it was too authoritarian and was later dropped.) McGuire (p. 98) explains the role of a leader in adding 'discernment' to prophecy so that individuals' prophecies do not get out of hand and disrupt the group.

6. D. Lehmann, *Struggle for the Spirit: Religious Transformation and Popular Culture in Brazil and Latin America*, Oxford: Polity Press 1996, pp. 210–14.

7. A. Chesnut, 'A preferential option for the spirit: the Catholic Charismatic renewal' in *Competitive Spirits: Latin America's New Religious Economy*, New York: OUP 2003 (forthcoming).

8. T. Hewitt, *Base Christian Communities and Social Change in Brazil*, London: University of Nebraska Press 1991; J. Burdick, *Looking for God in Brazil*, Berkeley: University of California Press 1994.

9. G. Davie, *Europe: The Exceptional Case: Parameters of Faith in the Modern World*, London: Darton, Longman and Todd 2002, p.19.

10. L. Iannacone, 'Introduction to the Economics of Religion', *Journal of Economic Literature*, 36 (3), 1997, pp. 1465–95.

11. P. Boyer, *Religion Explained: The Human Instincts that Fashion Gods, Spirits and Aancestors*, London: Heinemann 2001, pp. 275–76.

12. W. Christian, *Local Religion in Sixteenth Century Spain*, Princeton: Princeton University Press 1981.

13. A. Touraine, 'The Return of the Actor', *Social Research*, 52 (4),1985; M. Castells, *The Power of Identity*, Oxford: Blackwell 1997.

14. This is Portuguese for Pastoral Missions, or outreach work.

15. Castells, *The Power of Identity* (n.13) .

16. L. Boff, *Church: Charism and Power*, London: SCM Press and New York: Crossroad 1985. Boff is a very learned man who made path-breaking contributions to liberation theology. I suspect that he tired of this bookish activity and his output and activity from the mid-1980s became more closely tied to the ups and downs of church politics and Brazilian politics.

17. D. Lehmann, *Democracy and Development in Latin America: Economics, Politics and Religion in the Post-War Period*, Oxford: Polity Press 1990.

18. P. Birman, and D. Lehmann, 'Religion and the media in a battle for ideological hegemony', *Bulletin of Latin American Research*, 18 (2), 1999, pp. 145–64; A. Corten, *Pentecostalism in Brazil*, Basingstoke: Macmillan 1999; P. Birman, 'A mirror to the future: the media, evangelicals and politics in Brazil', paper pre-

sented to the seminar on Religion, Media and the Public Sphere, Amsterdam, December 2001.

19. Maranata is an Aramaic expression, used by St Paul in I Cor. 22 meaning 'Come O Lord' (NEB translation). (I am indebted to Alberto Melloni for this information.) The other names are taken from Csordas (op.cit., n. 4) and Neitz (op.cit., n. 4)

20. Though one parish priest told me he forbade them from using his church on the grounds that 'they believe in the private property of the Holy Spirit and I do not believe in private property'! (field research, 1991) .

21. Csordas, op. cit. (n.4), pp. 84–96 and 100–133.

22. MacGuire, op. cit. (n.4), p. 100

23. MacGuire, op. cit. (n.4), pp. 91–92

24. One observes similar patterns in Judaism, where ultra-Orthodox practices are penetrating the hitherto highly 'liberal' Reform community.

25. Birman, 'A mirror to the future' (n. 18); Birman and Lehmann , 'Religion and the media' (n. 18).

26. To underline the autonomy of these Conventions, I have been told that they have no compunction in extending their evangelizing into each other's notional territory. In other words, the state Convention is the highest level of management for Brazilian Assemblies.

27. See the www.iccrs.org website, which reproduces these figures from a 'World Christian Encyclopaedia' by David Barratt and Todd Johnson.

28. It is interesting in this connection to reflect on contrasting connotations of the word 'ecumenical'. In Csordas' book (n. 4) it is used to describe co-operation between charismatics and Pentecostals, yet in cosmopolitan parlance ecumenism is a liberal outlook which is utterly out of sympathy with charismatic and fundamentalist movements. In Latin America the followers of the People's Church would be highly ecumenical, having no problems in co-operating with Lutherans, Methodists etc. who tend to be theologically open-minded and anti-fundamentalist. Pentecostals and followers of the Charismatic Renewal in Latin America would regard ecumenism with extreme distrust.

29. R. de la Torre, 'The Catholic diocese: a transversalized institution', *Journal of Contemporary Religion*, 17 (3), 2002, pp. 303–16.

30. Ibid., p. 312.

31. Csordas, op. cit. (n. 4), pp. 114–24.

32. B. G. Dantas, *Vovó Nagô e Papai Branco*, Rio de Janeiro, Graal 1988.

33. A failed attempt is described in V. Boyer-Araujo, *Femmes et cultes de possession au Brésil: les compagnons invisibles*, Paris: L'Harmattan 1993.

34. D. Lehmann, 'Charisma and possession in Africa and Brazil', *Theory, Culture and Society*, 18 (5), 2001, pp. 45–74.

Contributors

ALBERTO MELLONI teaches contemporary history at the University of Modena and Reggio Emilia; he is a member of the XXIII Foundation for Religious Studies, Bologna, on the board of *Cristianesimo nella storia* and a member of the board of directors of *Concilium*. He has written extensively on the history and the institutions of Christianity from the Middle Ages (*Innocenzo IV*, preface by B. Tierney, Genoa 1990) to the twentieth century: he worked on John XXIII (*Tra Istanbul, Atene e la guerra. A. G. Roncalli vicario e delegato apostolico 1935–1944*, Genoa 1993; *Il Giornale dell'Anima di Giovanni XXIII,* Milan 2000), on Vatican II (as editor of the five volumes of *Storia del concilio Vaticano II diretta da G. Alberigo*, Bologna 1995–2001), on Vatican II diplomacy (*L'altra Roma. Politica e S. Sede durante il concilio Vaticano II, 1959–1965*, Bologna 2000), and on the conclave (*Il conclave. Storia di una instituzione*, Bologna 2001). His articles in different journals are devoted to the interplay between politics and religion.

Address: Via Crispi 6, 42100 Reggio Emilia, Italy
E-mail: alberto.melloni@tin.it

CLAUDIO GIANOTTO was born in 1950. He teaches Christian Origins at the Facoltà di lettere e filosofia of the University of Turin. His research fields are gnosticism, the history of biblical exegesis and interpretation and Jewish Christianity. His books include *Melchisedek e la sua tipologia*, Brescia 1984; *La testimonianza veritiera*, Brescia 1990; *Melchisédek (NH IX,1). Oblation, baptême et vision dans la gnose séthienne*, Leuven 2001 (with W.P. Funk and J.-P. Mahé); and *Verus Israel. Nuove prospettive sul giudeocristianesimo*, Paideia, Brescia 2001 (with G. Filoramo).

MATHIJS LAMBERIGTS was born in Belgium in 1955. He studied classical philology (MA) and church history and theology (PhD) at the Catholic

University of Leuven, where he has been Professor of Church History and theology since 1988. He has written around 100 articles on Augustine, the Pelagian Controversy, Augustinism and the Second Vatican Council, and has been the editor of around 10 books (on early church history, Augustinianism and the Second Vatican Council). He is a member of the Editiorial Board of the *History of Vatican II* (General Editor: G. Alberigo). Since 2000, he has been dean of the Faculty of Theology of the University.

Address: Faculteit Godgeleerdheid, K.U. Leuven, Sint-Michielsstraat 6, 3000 Leuven
E-mail: mathijs.lamberigts@theo.kuleuven.ac.be

ANDRÉ VAUCHEZ studied at the École Normale Supérieure and the École française de Rome. He was successively Professor of Mediaeval History at the universities of Rouen (1980–82) and Paris X-Nanterre (1983–95). Since September 1995, he has been Director of the École française de Rome d'archéologie et d'histoire. He has been Visiting Fellow at All Souls, Oxford (1986), and at the Institute for Advanced Study, Princeton (1991), and in 1996 was awarded the Ascoli prize for his historical work. He is editor of *Revue Mabillon (Revue internationale d'Histoire et de Littérature religieuses)*. His works are mainly on various aspects of mediaeval religious history, including popular religion, prophetic and charismatic currents and the history of spirituality. With C. Pietri (†), J.-M. Mayeur et M. Venard, he has edited the *Histoire du Christianisme* (14 vols), Paris 1990–2001, and with G. De Rosa and T. Gregory, the *Storia dell'Italia religiosa* (3 vols), Rome 1993–95.

Address: École française de Rome, Piazza Farnese, 67, I - 00186 Roma
E-mail: direction@ecole-francaise.it

ÉMILE POULAT is Director of Studies at the French Centre Nationale de la Recherche Scientifique (CNRS), founder of the group for the sociology of religion, and Director of Studies at the École des Hautes Études en Sciences Sociales (EHESS). Publications include: *Les cahiers manuscrits de Fourier*, Paris 1957; *Histoire, dogme et critique dans la crise moderniste*, Paris 1962; *Intégrisme et catholicisme intégral*, Paris 1969; *Église contre bourgeoisie*, Paris

1977; *Critique et mystique*, Paris 1984; *L'antimaçonnisme catholique*, Paris 1994.

Address: Rue Magenta 9bis, 5 park pavillon bleu, F-77300 Fontainebleau, France

ENZO PACE is Professor of Sociology and the Sociology of Religion at the Faculty of Political Sciences in the University of Padua. He is also Director of the Department of Sociology and President of the International Society for the Sociology of Religion. His main fields of research are the sociology of Islam, secularization and new religious movements. Recent publications include: *Sociologia dell' islam*, Rome 2001; *I fondamentalismi*, Rome and Bari 2002.

Address: Dept. of Sociology, via San Canziano 8, 35100 Padua
E-mail: vincenzo.pace@unip.it

ALEXANDRE GANOCZY was born in Budapest in 1928 and studied in Budapest, Paris and Rome, where he gained doctorates in philosophy and theology. He did research at the French Centre Nationale de la Recherche Scientifique (CNRS), and then was assistant at the Institute of Ecumenical Research in Tübingen. After that he taught dogmatic theology at the Institut Catholique in Paris and the University of Münster (1966–71). He was Ordinarius Professor of Dogmatics at the University of Würzburg from 1972 to 1996. He has been awarded honorary doctorates by the universities of Geneva (1983) and Budapest (1990). His main works include: *Calvin, théologien de l'Eglise et du ministère* (1964); *Le jeune Calvin* (1966); *Der schöpferische Mensch und die Schöpfung Gottes* (1976); *Schöpfungslehre* (?1987); *Einführung in die katholische. Sakramentenlehre* (1979, ?1991), *Einführung in die Dogmatik* (1983); *Suche nach Gott auf den Wegen der Natur* (1992); *Chaos, Zufall, Schöpfungsglaube* (1995); *Unendliche Weiten. Naturwissenschaftliches Weltbild und christlicher Glaube* (1998); *Der Dreinige Schöpfer. Versuch einer theologischen Synergetik* (2001).

Address: Campagne Saye, F-04 300 Dauphin, France
E-mail : ALEXANDRE.GANOCZY@wanadoo.fr

JEAN-PAUL DURAND OP is professor at the Institut catholique in Paris, and chief editor of the *Revue d'éthique et de théologie morale*. A canon lawyer and moralist, he was dean of the Faculty of Canon Law at the Institut between 1992 and 2001; in 1995 he founded the international consortium 'Droit canonique et culture' and he has been co-director of the centre 'Droit et sociétés religieuses' since 1992. He is author of a three-volume work on *La liberté des congrégations religieuses en France*, Paris 1999, and a small volume on *Les institutions religieuses*, Paris 1999.

E-mail: jp.durand@editionsducerf.fr

LUCA DIOTALLEVI was born at Terni, Italy, in 1959. He graduated in philosophy at the 'La Sapienza' University in Rome and gained his PhD in sociology at the Università degli Studi in Parma. He teaches sociology at the Facoltà di Scienze della Formazione dell'Università di Roma Tre. He has been senior fellow at the Center for the Study of World Religions of Harvard Divinity School. Recent publications include *Il rompicapo della secolarizzazione italiana*, Catanzaro 2002; 'Italian Case and American Theories: Refining Secularization Paradigm', *Sociology of Religion* 63/2, 2002.

Address: Università di Roma Tre, Facoltà di Scienze della Formazione, via dei Mille, 23 (I piano, stanza 7), 00185 Rome, Italy
E-mail: l.diotallevi@educ.uniroma3.it.

DAVID LEHMANN is a social scientist at Cambridge University. He has worked extensively in Latin America on development and on religion. He is the author of *Democracy and Development in Latin America* (1990), and *Struggle for the Spirit: Popular Culture and Religious Transformation in Brazil and Latin America* (1996). More recently he has undertaken research on ethnic and religious renewal among Israel's Sephardi Jewish population.

Address: Faculty of Social and Political Sciences, Free School Lane, Cambridge CB2 3RQ
E-mail: adl1@cam.ac.uk

Concilium Subscription Information

Forthcoming issues in 2003

February 2003/1: *Rethinking Martyrdom*
Edited by Teresa Okure, Jon Sobrino and Felix Wilfred

April 2003/2: *The Discourse of Human Dignity*
Edited by Regina Ammicht-Quinn, Maureen Junker
Kenny and Elsa Tamez

June 2003/3: *Movements in the Church*
Edited by Alberto Melloni

October 2003/4: *Learning from other Faiths*
Edited by Hermann Häring, Janet Martin Soskice and
Felix Wilfred

December 2003/5: *Reconciliation in a World of Conflicts*
Edited by Luis Carlos Susin, Maria Pilar Aquino and Jon
Sobrino

New subscribers: to receive *Concilium 2003* (five issues) anywhere in the world, please copy this form, complete it in block capitals and send it with your payment to the address below.

Please enter my subscription for *Concilium 2003*

Individuals
____ £29.00 UK/Rest of World
____ $57.00 North America

Institutions
____ £48.50 UK/Rest of World
____ $93.50 North America

Please add £15.00/$22.50 for airmail delivery

Payment Details:
Payment must accompany all orders and can be made by cheque or credit card
I enclose a cheque for £/$ _____ Payable to SCM-Canterbury Press Ltd
Please charge my Visa/MasterCard (Delete as appropriate) for £/$ _____
Credit card number ....
Expiry date ....
Signature of cardholder ....
Name on card ....
Telephone .... E-mail ....

Send your order to *Concilium*, SCM-Canterbury Press Ltd
9–17 St Albans Place, London N1 ONX, UK
Tel +44 (0)20 7359 8033 Fax +44 (0)20 7359 0049
E-Mail: office@scm-canterburypress.co.uk

Customer service information:
All orders must be prepaid. Subscriptions are entered on an annual basis (i.e. January to December) No refunds on subscriptions will be made after the first issue of the Journal has been despatched. If you have any queries or require information about other payment methods, please contact our Customer services department.